Dedicated to

J. Mumma for nurturing a life-long passion for geography, but also to the people of the world whose lives are constrained by the invisible lines drawn by others.

GAMES OF LIFE AND LAND

A comparative analysis of the origins of true enclaves in South and Central Asia, their impacts on public policy, and factors prolonging their existence

Glen R. Hamburg

Institute of Foreign Policy Studies (IFPS)

Centre for Pakistan and West Asian Studies (CPWAS)

Calcutta University
Kolkata

in association with

KNOWLEDGE WORLD

KW Publishers Pvt Ltd
New Delhi

2011 FPBA BEST PUBLISHERS AWARD (ENGLISH)

The Court of Directors of the East India Company sent a despatch in July, 1854 to the Governor-General of India in Council, suggesting the establishment of the Universities of Calcutta, Madras and Bombay. In pursuance of that despatch, the University of Calcutta was founded on January 24, 1857. The University adopted in the first instance, the pattern of the University of London and gradually introduced modifications in its constitution.

The Institute of Foreign Policy Studies (IFPS) at the University of Calcutta is an autonomous centre devised for the study of international relations, with particular emphasis on foreign policy. Funded by the Ministry of External Affairs (MEA), Government of India, the institute purports to create a pool of foreign policy specialists capable of offering advice on matters pertaining to India's international relations. The Institute has already been earmarked for developing regional expertise with reference to the Government of India's Look East Policy, and that towards West Asia. The IFPS has also been chosen as one of the ten centres for United Nations Academic Initiative, functioning as the hub for studies on peace and conflict resolution.

The Centre for Pakistan and West Asian Studies, Calcutta University, was set up in 2005 under the UGC Area Studies Programme. It is the only research outfit associated with a University in eastern India with an exclusive focus on Pakistan and West Asian countries, Afghanistan, Iran and Iraq in particular, which together constitute a part of India's extended neighbourhood in the West. The Centre, since its establishment in 2005, has tried to develop a greater understanding of this extended neighbourhood by looking at the internal dynamics of the region with far greater detail than is generally accorded by other area studies outfits in the country.

ISBN 978-93-83649-00-6

Published in India by Kalpana Shukla

KNOWLEDGE WORLD

KW Publishers Pvt Ltd
4676/21, First Floor, Ansari Road, Daryaganj, New Delhi 110002
✆ +91.11.23263498/43528107 ✉ knowledgeworld@vsnl.net • www.kwpub.com

Printed and Bound in India

Contents

Introduction

There are areas of the globe where tiny pieces of one country are quite literally stuck inside of another. The pieces are called true enclaves and with more than 200 such sites of strange political geography, Asia has the most in the world. By far the majority of these lie along India's border with northern Bangladesh where, according to common accounts, a vast complex of enclaves is the result of some reckless gambling way back in the eighteenth century. It is said that a local Maharajah and a Mughal prince heedlessly wagered between themselves their holdings of small, disconnected tracks of land just as poker players bet, swap, and squander their chips. When one of the rulers lost, he simply handed some fields over to the other, the boundaries of which eventually became those separating India and Bangladesh today. There are more enclaves half-way across the continent in Central Asia, these often said to be the design of a crafty dictator, Joseph Stalin, who was keen to knot together ethnic groups with purposefully illogical borders that divided, conquered, and complicated any efforts toward local independence.

Such games and conscious tactics, say many, led to what are surely the two most geographically complex border regions anywhere on the planet, wherein mass shards of one country are lodged like cartographic shrapnel in the body of a neighbour. Yet despite these stories being kept alive in the narratives of area residents—and frequently cited as fact by journalists, academics, and politicians—they are but myths, the true historical origins of the South and Central Asian enclaves being more convoluted and less sudden, though no less intriguing. Sure, it is fair to say that a relative few played a role in their initial creation. But, the biographies of these enclaves read that their continued existence is the fault of so many others. They have used these spots of land for decades as ante in their often unrelated domestic and international contests over natural resources, business interests, regional security, group identity, and electoral advantage. In this way, Asia's enclaves seem to have become the very wagers and game pieces that popular mythology says they were originally meant to be.

Yet while apparently beneficial to some, the enclaves have had a profoundly negative effect on the people who actually live in or near them. To be sure, the very existence of these geographic features in South and Central Asia has left tens of thousands of people dangerously vulnerable, effectively stateless, and truly trapped. They are dens of lawlessness and the sparks of communal conflict, nexuses of neglect and the seeds of strife. It has been widely acknowledged that in order to solve these most pressing issues of human security—and of human dignity—the enclaves must be dissolved by merging them with the principal territory by which they are surrounded. But year after year, decade after decade, they remain. They do surely then have some worth to someone.

The literature is rich in discussions of the origins of both the South and Central Asian enclaves, but accounts are widely inconsistent. This paper will clarify how these enclaves came about and argue that an accurate understanding of their history is important to the process of drawing new political geographies in South Asia, Central Asia, and elsewhere. It will then argue that international enclaves frustrate the expressed policy goals and assumed public interests in India and Kyrgyzstan, but that competing agendas in both countries nonetheless prolong their existence. Before any of this discussion, however, it is useful to define relevant terminology and to describe the location and general characteristics of the case study enclaves in both regions.

CHAPTER ONE

Defining Terms Through Comparative Geography

Nearly everything about the places discussed in this paper seems contested, from the exact number of enclaves in South and Central Asia to the number of people who live in them, from their historical origins to the motives which keep them alive. Even the definition of the word enclave seems up for debate.

Take for example descriptions of the tiny yet independent European state of San Marino, which is entirely surrounded by the territory of Italy. For decades San Marino has been casually referred to in the media and by scholars of varying disciplines as an "enclave" (Panico, 2009, p. 403; *The Globe and Mail*, 1982, p. 11; *The New York Times*, 1959, p. 38). So has the independent state of Lesotho, a sovereign kingdom which lies fully within the territory of South Africa, by Reina (1993, p. 26) and Epprecht (1995, p. 323) more recently. The Nakhchivan Autonomous Republic, a portion of sovereign Azerbaijan, is physically separated from its "home country" and sandwiched between the territories of Armenia, Turkey, and Iran. In reporting on the development of West Asian energy infrastructure in 2010, the Xinhua News Agency termed this obscure piece of land an "enclave" as well. Other places which are detached from their country's principal territory, yet not entirely landlocked, have even been referred to as "enclaves," such as Spain's Melilla (Cembalest, 1997, p. 9), the United States' Point Roberts (McAllister, 1996, p. A3), and Russia's Kaliningrad Oblast (Das Kundu, 2003, p. 626).

Geographers, however, should and generally do use the term more judiciously, ascribing to it a particular definition that sets true enclaves apart from these only similar situations. And a distinction between such cases really does matter, especially in comparative analyses of the opportunities and challenges that a location's political geography poses to the people who live in it, to the officials who govern it, and to the foreign neighbours who surround or sit beside it.

Consider Melilla, which clings to the northern rim of the African continent some 60 kilometres south across the Mediterranean Sea from the Spanish "mainland" (*The Economist*, 2002). The territory shares a land border only with Morocco (see Map 1 of the Maps Annex). But because Melilla also has a coastline, its residents, goods, and resources can transit easily by ferry to their country's principal territory in Europe without crossing any troublesome international boundary. This is a critical detail. Spain is not reliant on Morocco to grant it access to its territory, as it might be if Melilla was entirely encased within foreign Moroccan lands. With direct access to the sea, Melillans and their Spanish government need not necessarily be concerned with how the government of Morocco might choose to restrict the transit of people and goods, say, with punitive immigration or customs policies. They could simply go around.

Lesotho, shown in Map 2, does not have such geographic luxury and nor do the two other countries in the world, San Marino and the Vatican City, whose total territory is completely surrounded by that of just one other state. Farran (1955) only alludes to these countries' potential vulnerability, but it should be quite apparent. A "host state" could choose to restrict the movement of goods, services, and people across its lands to any state lying within its outer boundaries, thus compelling the inner states to rely on their host's benevolence so as not to be the victim of a kind of blockade.

Cobbe (1988) considers such possibilities in his review of the history of economic relations between Lesotho and surrounding South Africa. He notes that with Lesotho's heavy reliance on income from migrants working in South African mines in the 1970s and 1980s, and with its reliance on imported goods originating from or at least transiting through South Africa, changes in South Africa's immigration or customs policies could have had dramatic effects on Lesotho's economy. From this perspective, policymakers in Lesotho at the time would likely have been advised to maintain good relations with South Africa in order to ensure their country's economic prosperity, given its political geography.

Yet Cobbe also points out that Lesotho's position "is to some extent a vulnerability that is so total as to be unexploitable by [the South African capital] Pretoria" in practice (p. 76), arguing that any major disruption in the economy of Lesotho by South Africa could cause hardship and instability that eventually spills over into South African territory. Indeed, a host must be wary that another state within its territory does not fester into a blister.

Now to Nakhchivan in the Caucasus region of Eurasia. The Nakhchivan Autonomous Republic is a separated subnational unit of the sovereign state of Azerbaijan, just as Melilla is of Spain. It is also similar to Lesotho because it is entirely landlocked. But Nakhchivan differs from both these cases in its number of foreign neighbours, which in turn affects its residents' and its country's well-being. As Map 3, Nakhchivan is bordered by Iran and Turkey to the southwest and cleaved from its "homeland" by Armenia—a country Azerbaijan is still technically at war with (Hoggarth, 2012)—to the northeast. One might assume Nakhchivan's physical separation from principal Azerbaijani territory (by a hostile neighbour, no less) and its landlocked position would present certain difficulties for its residents and the Azerbaijani state. In fact, the country's Ministry of Foreign Affairs admits that it does (Republic of Azerbaijan Ministry of Foreign Affairs, n.d.). Though as Baghirov (2012) counters, its geopolitical position could also present certain opportunities to Azerbaijan as well. The territory after all acts as a kind of satellite, allowing the rest of the country better access to foreign markets such as Turkey, which the principal territory of Azerbaijan does not share a common border with (Efendiev, 1999; News.az, 2012; Republic of Azerbaijan Ministry of Foreign Affairs, n.d.).

Melilla, Lesotho, and the Nakhchivan Autonomous Republic are no doubt curious instances of political geography which pose unique challenges and opportunities to their residents, economies, and governments. They are, however, not what are termed by geographers as true enclaves. Nor are San Marino or the Vatican City, or even Point Roberts or Kaliningrad Oblast (see Maps 4, 5, and 6). Rather, as the geographers Farran (1955), Vinokurov (2007), van Schendel (2002), and Whyte (2002) explain, a true enclave is a piece of one state's territory entirely surrounded by the territory of just one other state. Nakhchivan is not an enclave because it is bordered by more than one foreign state.[1] It is an exclave of Azerbaijan, though, because it is physically detached from its country's principal territory and can only be accessed from elsewhere in Azerbaijan after crossing at least one international boundary (Vinokurov, 2007). Lesotho is referred to as an enclaved state and not a true enclave because all, instead of just a portion, of its sovereign territory is surrounded by South Africa. Lastly, Melilla is neither an enclave nor an exclave because it is not surrounded by the territory of another state, and therefore can be accessed from the Spanish mainland without crossing any international boundary.

These definitions and conventions are used here in this paper in order to highlight and more effectively compare the unique circumstances of true enclaves in two regions of Asia. Such an approach will help demonstrate that it is the particular positioning of these areas—that is, being physically separated from home territory and completely enclosed in the territory of one foreign state—which creates great adversity for some, but also some lucrative advantages for others which inevitably prolong their existence. Note that all true enclaves (from here forward simply "enclave") are by definition also exclaves with respect to their home state. For example, Barak, the piece of sovereign Kyrgyz territory inside of Uzbekistan, is termed an exclave of Kyrgyzstan because it is separated from its home country's principal territory. But it is also an enclave of Uzbekistan, the country which surrounds it. This paper uses either the term enclave or exclave as appropriate given the syntactical circumstance.

1. The entirety of the Nakhchivan Autonomous Republic is not an enclave respective to the principal territory of Azerbaijan. However, the subnational unit of Azerbaijan does itself have jurisdiction over a piece of territory that is enclave, the village of Tigranashen. Tigranashen is part of Azerbaijan's Nakhchivan Autonomous Republic, but physically detached from it by about five kilometres and entirely surrounded by the sovereign territory of Armenia. Tigranashen is a true enclave and an exclave of both Azerbaijan and the Nakhchivan Autonomous Republic.

CHAPTER TWO

Locating and Counting Case Study Enclaves

At the foot of the Himalaya, tea plantations slope into a disorientingly vast expanse of swampy rice and jute fields. Tigers are said to lurk in the nearby forests, mosquitoes swarm the heavy skies. It is here, along the southern edge of a thin stretch of Indian land separating Bhutan from Bangladesh, that you will find the world's largest collection of true enclaves (Map 7). The majority of these enclaves are exclaves of India surrounded by Bangladeshi territory and the rest are Bangladeshi exclaves surrounded by Indian territory.

Perplexingly though, while the location of each enclave is fully known, charted, and recognised by the Indian and Bangladeshi governments (Jones, 2009; van Schendel, 2002; Whyte, 2002), the exact number of enclaves is regularly misreported. In fact Whyte (2002) chronicles two dozen different counts by researchers, journalists, and government officials between the years 1936 and 2001. But the misreporting has continued since, with both Ghosh (2013) and Sarkar (2013) erroneously citing 111 Indian exclaves in Bangladesh and 51 exclaves of Bangladesh in India. Poplin (2013) finds just 102 Indian and 71 Bangladeshi exclaves, while *The Economist* (2011) claims there to be a combined total of 201.

To be clear, there are 106 Indian exclaves inside of Bangladesh and 92 Bangladeshi exclaves surrounded by the Indian state of West Bengal, for a total of 198 true enclaves between the two countries (Jones, 2009, p. 373; Vinokurov, 2007, p. 24; Whyte, 2002, p. 6).

Whyte (2002) considers the miscounts to originate in a confusion between the word "enclave" and the native terms for local administrative units, such as "chhitmahal," which may encompass multiple separate enclaves or divide a single enclave. The others' figures may also come from a misunderstanding of the provisions of related land transfer agreements. Further, he also respects that the general "complexity of the boundary" (p. 428) may even be contributing to the varied figures, inasmuch suggesting that the India–Bangladesh border is so convoluted that those studying it, reporting on it, and tasked with governing it themselves have difficulty keeping track of just whose lands are whose.

Surely compounding this geographic complexity is the fact that some of the 198 enclaves are actually inside of others. India possesses three such second-order enclaves (also termed "counter-enclaves") within Bangladeshi enclaves, and 21 Bangladeshi enclaves are actually inside of other Indian fragments. The world's only third-order enclave (or "counter-counter-enclave") is also sovereign Indian territory. In other words, there's an Indian enclave within a Bangladeshi enclave within an Indian enclave within the principal territory of Bangladesh (Whyte, 2002). Table 1 below summarises these counts.

Table 1: Number and positioning of South Asian enclaves by state (Jones, 2009; Vinokurov, 2007; Whyte, 2002)

	India	Bangladesh
First-order enclaves:	102	71
Second-order enclaves:	3	21
Third-order enclaves:	1	0
Total enclaves:	106	92

In total, approximately 17,200 acres of exclaved Indian territory is enclaved by Bangladesh and nearly 12,300 acres of exclaved Bangladeshi territory is enclaved by India, of which one unit is as large as 4,617 acres and another as small as .27 acres (Vinokurov, 2007; Whyte, 2002). It is not at all clear how Chaudhury (2011) calculated that "almost 3,000 acres of Bangladesh's land lies in India and India has around 3,500 acres inside Bangladesh." Many other recent reports, including those by Sarkar (2013), *The Hindu* (2013), and New Delhi Television Limited (2011), state that only about 7,000 acres of land within India's main boundaries belongs to Bangladesh. These figures likely omit the roughly 5,000-acre exclave of Bangladesh known as Dahagram-Angarpota, the only enclave that would not be transferred according to the terms of the agreement ratified by Bangladesh in 1974 and currently being considered by India.

Another reason Dahagram-Angarpota may not be included in some figures of enclave area is Bangladeshi residents of the territory are officially permitted to transit across the surrounding Indian territory to the Bangladeshi mainland through a 175-metre strip known as the Tin Bigha Corridor, which since 2011 is open 24 hours a day (Bhasin, 2011; Cons, 2012; Jones, 2009; *The Daily Star*, 2011). The corridor, as explained by an Indian Border Security Forces (BSF) commander in a June 2013 interview,[2] is fenced on all sides and its traffic controlled by Indian BSF officers who ensure that Dahagram-Angarpota's residents only pass east and west through the corridor while Indian residents pass north and south (Map 8). The arrangement thus keeps the enclave's roughly 16,000 people (Jones, 2009) connected by what van Schendel (2002, p. 139) calls an "umbilical cord" to their home country, while at the same time ensuring that the residents of Indian territory southwest of the Dahagram-Angarpota and east of the Teesta River are not cut off by the corridor from their own homelands (van Schendel, 2002; Whyte, 2002).

But even with this special arrangement made to local residents, Dahagram-Angarpota is still technically a true enclave. The Tin Bigha Corridor remains under Indian sovereignty and is operated by Indian officials (Bhasin, 2011; van Schendel, 2002). And however unlikely, the Indian government could, if it wished, choose to sever that umbilical cord by cancelling the agreement and blocking traffic through the corridor, thus leaving the Bangladeshis in Dahagram-Angarpota marooned. Because of Dahagram-Angarpota's political geography, its residents are still subject to India's graces, just as the residents of Bangladesh's 91 other exclaves are.

2. The interview was conducted in Kolkata, India in English on June 6, 2013. Because the interviewee did not have express permission from superiors to participate in the interview, the interviewee's name has not been included. However, a full transcript of the interview is available at the Institute of Foreign Policy Studies, University of Calcutta in Kolkata, India.

There are far fewer enclaves among the craggy hills and fertile valleys of Central Asia, but they are shared by three states: Kyrgyzstan, Tajikistan, and Uzbekistan. These enclaves are caught in a net of national boundaries so twisted up that it is difficult to see on a map of the region where one of these countries ends and another begins (Map 9).

Unlike in South Asia where the exact number of enclaves is known (albeit frequently misreported) and where the enclave boundaries are accepted and charted, the number of Central Asian enclaves seems up for debate, with even the boundaries of the confirmed ones far from settled. Jafarova (2013), Vinokurov (2007), and Whyte (2002) all cite eight total enclaves in Central Asia, but only the latter two geographers identify them by name. One exclave of Tajikistan referred to by two different names is said to lie within Uzbekistan, while another two exclaves of Tajikistan can be found in Kyrgyzstan. They identify just four Uzbek enclaves inside of Kyrgyzstan and one enclave of Kyrgyzstan (the village of Barak), within the principal territory of Uzbekistan. Table 2 lists the "home state" (the sovereign country) of the enclaves and its "host state" (the state within which the enclave is located), as well as the names or general location of the enclave, all according to Vinokurov (2007, p. 5) and Whyte (2002, pp. 24-25).

Table 2: Central Asian enclaves according to Whyte (2002, p. 5) and Vinokurov (2007, pp. 24-25)

Home State	Host State	Enclave Names or General Location
Tajikistan	Uzbekistan	Sarvaksoi or Sarvaki-bolo
Tajikistan	Kyrgyzstan	Vorukh
Tajikistan	Kyrgyzstan	Kairagach or Western Qalcha
Uzbekistan	Kyrgyzstan	Kalacha
Uzbekistan	Kyrgyzstan	Sokh
Uzbekistan	Kyrgyzstan	Dzhangail
Uzbekistan	Kyrgyzstan	Shakhimardan or Iordan
Kyrgyzstan	Uzbekistan	Barak

Vinokurov and Whyte have both done extensive, reliable research of the world's enclaves and their works, along with those of van Schendel, are rightly considered some of the most authoritative in the field. However, it is possible that they, Jafarova (2013), and others have overlooked a ninth enclave in Central Asia. Frustratingly though, those who identify a ninth true enclave in the region do not even agree where or whose it is. The geography of the region is that contested, that complex.

Kokaisl and Kokaislová (2009, p. 137), for example, list Kairagach and Western Qalcha as two separate exclaves of Tajikistan within Kyrgyzstan, not one piece of territory with two different names as figured by Vinokurov (2007) and Whyte (2002). Their enumeration of the region's enclaves is shown here in Table 3.

Table 3: Central Asian enclaves according to Kokaisl and Kokaislová (2009, p. 137)

Home State	Host State	Enclave Name or General Location
Tajikistan	Uzbekistan	Sarvan or Saravaksoi
Tajikistan	Kyrgyzstan	Vorukh
Tajikistan	Kyrgyzstan	Kairagach
Tajikistan	Kyrgyzstan	Western Qalcha
Uzbekistan	Kyrgyzstan	Chong Kara or Kalacha
Uzbekistan	Kyrgyzstan	Sokh-Tayan
Uzbekistan	Kyrgyzstan	Djangail or Khalmion
Uzbekistan	Kyrgyzstan	Shakhimardan
Kyrgyzstan	Uzbekistan	Barak or Barak-ail

The International Crisis Group (ICG) (2002) reports having travelled throughout the region and conducting interviews with local officials concerning the enclaves. ICG has also determined that there are nine enclaves in Central Asia, but not the same nine as Kokaisl and Kokaislová (2009). Rather ICG (pp. 4-5) says there are just seven enclaves in Kyrgyzstan: two belonging to Tajikistan and "the remainder to Uzbekistan." One of the two Tajikistan-owned enclaves, ICG says (pp. 4 and 19), is the village of Vorokh and the other "a very small" enclave called Western Qalcha. Khamidov (2003) and the Jamestown Foundation (2013) agree that there are only two exclaves of Tajikistan in Kyrgyzstan, Vorukh and Western Qalcha. The Jamestown Foundation concurs with ICG's determination that there are five exclaves of Uzbekistan in

Kyrgyzstan. The total of Central Asian enclaves as identified by ICG is listed in Table 4, and the total according to the Jamestown Foundation in Table 5.

Table 4: Central Asian enclaves according to International Crisis Group (2002, pp. 4-5)

Home State	Host State	Enclave Name or General Location
Tajikistan	Uzbekistan	A small, but unnamed enclave
Tajikistan	Kyrgyzstan	Vorukh[3]
Tajikistan	Kyrgyzstan	Western Qalacha[4]
Uzbekistan	Kyrgyzstan	Sokh
Uzbekistan	Kyrgyzstan	Shahimardan
Uzbekistan	Kyrgyzstan	A small, but unnamed enclave
Uzbekistan	Kyrgyzstan	A small, but unnamed enclave
Uzbekistan	Kyrgyzstan	A small, but unnamed enclave
Kyrgyzstan	Uzbekistan	Barak

Table 5: Central Asian enclaves according to the Jamestown Foundation (2013)

Home State	Host State	Enclave Name or General Location
Tajikistan	Uzbekistan	Sarvan
Tajikistan	Kyrgyzstan	Vorukh
Tajikistan	Kyrgyzstan	Kaigarach or Western Qalacha
Uzbekistan	Kyrgyzstan	Sokh
Uzbekistan	Kyrgyzstan	Sakhimardan
Uzbekistan	Kyrgyzstan	Qalacha
Uzbekistan	Kyrgyzstan	Dzhangail
Uzbekistan	Kyrgyzstan	Tayan
Kyrgyzstan	Uzbekistan	Barak

In response to a request for clarification from the Embassy of Kyrgyzstan in Washington, DC the embassy's First Secretary conceded that determining the number of foreign enclaves within the principal boundaries of his country was "really not an easy question" (Adanov,

3. Note that this is a different transliteration of the enclave's name than that referenced by others. In the Tajik alphabet, the name for this territory is written as Bopyx.
4. This is also a different, though more-often used transliteration.

2013). Nonetheless, the First Secretary found that the official website for the government of Batken Oblast, one of the seven subnational administrative units of the country, cites Batken territory surrounding just six foreign enclaves. Two, which the First Secretary calls "Kayragach" and "Vorukh," are said to belong to Tajikistan. The four others, "Sokh," "Shakhimardan," "Chon Gara," and "Tash Dobe," belong to Uzbekistan (Adanov, 2013).[5]

According to a representative of the Embassy of the United States in Dushanbe, no other countries have exclaves in Tajikistan, however the representative is aware of just two Tajik exclaves, Vorukh and a place called Chorku. The embassy representative was unaware of other possible Tajik exclaves in Uzbekistan and Kyrgyzstan, simply stating that border delineations with the latter country "is not complete" (Jacobs, 2013).

Aydarov (2009) also refers to the Tajik community of Chorku north of Vorukh as an "enclave." However, maps of the region, including one published in a special report of this and neighbouring communities by the Jamoat Resource Centre of Vorukh (2011, p. 3) available through the United Nations Development Programme in Tajikistan, show that Chorku is not a true enclave; it is connected by a thin finger of territory to principal Tajikistan and not entirely surrounded by the sovereign lands of Kyrgyzstan (or any other state).

Representatives of Uzbekistan have not responded to inquiries into which foreign enclaves it has within its territory, or those which it claims in neighbouring states. The US Embassy in Tashkent has stated that it is "not in a position to substantiate the existence" of a ninth, small enclave south of and separate from Sokh (Padgett, 2013).

With such disagreement among reputable researchers, on-the-ground organisations, and government representatives, this paper cannot definitively say how many enclaves there are in Central Asia. It can nonetheless be assumed that there are at least eight and possibly nine true enclaves between Kyrgyzstan, Tajikistan, and Uzbekistan, the

5. A copy of the email correspondence with First Secretary Adanov is available through the Institute of Foreign Policy Studies, University of Calcutta in Kolkata, India.

majority of which lie within the principal territory of Kyrgyzstan. It is also certain that there is only one exclave of Kyrgyzstan, the village of Barak located in eastern Uzbekistan (Ibbotson & Lovell-Hoare, 2010; International Crisis Group, 2002; IRIN News Service, 2005; Kimsanov, 2003; Kokaisl & Kokaislová, 2009; Vinokurov, 2007; Whyte, 2002).

Of both the agreed to and disputed exclave of Uzbekistan within Kyrgyzstan, Sokh is by far the largest. According to Maynes (2003) it encompasses about 80,000 acres, though Whyte (2002) says it is less than 60,000. Utyaganova (2001) cites it as less than 30,000 acres. The disparity most likely stems from the fact that the precise boundaries of the Central Asian enclaves have not been formally delimited or fully demarcated on the ground, their limits being widely—and often violently—disputed between Central Asian states, as this paper will later discuss (International Crisis Group, 2002; Jafarova, 2013; Megoran, 2012; Pylenko, 2005; Rahimov & Urezaeva, 2005). So predictably, there also are some sources which say Kyrgyzstan's exclave, Barak, in Uzbekistan is about 470 acres in size (Vinokurov, 2007; Whyte, 2002), yet still others who say it is almost 1,000 acres (AKIpress News Agency, 2013).

The ambiguous, indeed hotly contested nature of the enclaves' edges in Central Asia should be contrasted with the conclusively defined and mutually accepted boundaries of the enclaves in South Asia, for such a comparison shows how the degrees to which enclave boundaries are agreed to and honoured by the respective governments, and known to the people living near them, can determine conditions for individual, national, and regional security. Challengingly though, the divergent qualities of enclave boundaries can lead to certain opportunities and adverse consequences.

Here are three examples of this tension. First, an unmarked boundary between hostile neighbours can create terrifying consequences for enclave residents who inadvertently stray across them, as will be demonstrated in Section Four of this paper. Yet the known and respected boundary of an anomalous enclave can also be exploited by enterprising criminals or even terrorists. Second, there are some who say demarcating enclave boundaries facilitates or is even a prerequisite for any talks of exchanging troublesome enclave territory between states. But as South Asia has demonstrated, knowing for certain that there is an imbalance in land area can also complicate such negotiations and serve as convenient leverage in unrelated, distracting colloquies. Thirdly, tenebrous or erratic enclave boundaries can lead to communal or cross-national violence, though as Sahlins (1998) has shown, the fixing of boundaries can also engender new conceptions of group identity that did not exist before, conceptions that might feed new conflicts entirely.

This paper will be reflecting on such conflicting opportunities and consequences in Section Four with a look at how political geography affects the living conditions of those in South and Central Asia's enclaves, and how the enclaves are (or should be) connected with other domestic and international interests. But before proceeding with these analyses, it is important to clarify one other commonly-distorted part of the discourse on enclaves in South and Central Asia: how their troublesome political geographies came to be in the first place.

CHAPTER THREE

(A)historical Origins

Perhaps the most commonly repeated explanation among journalists for the origins of the enclaves in South Asia is the story of those partying princes playing poker (though some say they played chess). Really, it seems most every news article covering the living conditions of enclave residents and the ongoing enclave land transfer discussions between India and Bangladesh make reference of some kind to this story (*Deccan Herald*, 2011; New Delhi Television Limited, 2011; Sattar, 2012; *The Arunachal Pioneer*, 2013). Karim (2011) doubles down on the academic legitimacy of the gambling legend, writing for the *Daily Star*:

> "Historians say these territories were part of high stake card or chess games between the kings of Cooch Behar and Rangpur and handed over to each other in payment for the gambling debts."

Unfortunately, Karim does not detail which "historians" have uncovered these circumstances to be true, nor do any of the other journalists who make this fascinating claim.

As mentioned in the introduction, the gambling explanation is a myth, one unsubstantiated by—in fact contrary to—the known history of the region. Yet its constant repetition as not only endearing tale, but proven fact, indicates that the media coverage of the South Asian enclaves takes place in an echo chamber of rumour, misunderstanding, and general carelessness.

Another explanation that gets tossed about—and sometimes confusingly combined with the gambling myth—is that a British geographer named Cyril Radcliffe either purposefully set out to create the enclave boundaries at the dusk of the British Raj, or that he sort of just ended up drawing them accidentally in a sloppy, frantic effort to partition India and Pakistan in 1947. One of these versions of the Radcliffe explanation finds its way into many circles. The Asiatic Society of Bangladesh, for example, published in its 2006 encyclopaedia of Bangladesh-related topics the following:

> "The problem of enclaves belonging to India and Bangladesh is the result of both history and geography. Just before the partition of Bengal 1947, a Boundary Commission, headed by Sir Cyril Radcliffe, was appointed according to the Mountbatten Plan of 3 June 1947, to divide Bengal and Punjab between India and Pakistan. The Mountbatten timetable for independence was a crash programme and required that the boundary demarcation should be carried out 'with the greatest speed' ... Injustice and great hardship could not be avoided, and the awards themselves were sure to be unpopular and to become the subject of controversy. Because of the whimsical execution of the award, enclaves on both sides of the border exist as unresolvable problems even today. In a situation of inactivity of the members of the commission, zamindars, nawabs, local leaders, and even owners of tea estates of both Hindu and Muslim communities are said to have influenced working out of the award in Bengal in their own interests with fair and foul means. Bangladesh has thus inherited the enclave problem created by the British during partition in 1947."

Acclaimed writer and journalist Haroon Habib has a similar interpretation of the origins of the enclaves in South Asia, writing in the *Hindu* in November 2011:

> "The issue of the [South Asia] enclaves is the result of a hasty and unwise job done by the Boundary Commission led by Sir Cyril Radcliffe in 1947—the year British India was partitioned."

A leader of what is likely the foremost organisation advocating an exchange of enclave territory between India and Bangladesh was asked by the author of this paper in May 2013 how he and those living in the enclaves understood the history. He answered, with some contradiction, that in fact he believed both of these stories to be true, that the enclaves were the unfortunate result of some gambling and that an "irresponsible" Cyril Radcliffe "deliberately" created the enclave boundaries in the lead up to India's independence in 1947. What motive, not to mention time, this supposedly harried and rushed Radcliffe could have had to intentionally create such complex boundaries—even a third-order enclave only 1.7 acres in size with no residents—the activist leader did not explain. But he did insist that the enclave residents also understood the history of their own geography, a geography which the activist leader says has caused such "suffering," just the same as he did (Sengupta, 2013, p. 6).

In fact Radcliffe needed neither motive nor sufficient time to draw up the enclave boundaries—because that was not his job. Radcliffe and his commission played no part in the creation of the South Asia enclaves. Those exclaves of India now stuck inside of Bangladesh did not become sovereign territory of the Republic of India until 1949, years after Radcliffe and the British colonialists left the Subcontinent (van Schendel, 2002; van Schendel, 2005; Whyte, 2002).

The year the South Asian enclaves were actually born is 1713. In the decades prior, the region where the enclaves now lie was the setting for tedious battles between the Mughals and the Kingdom of Cooch Behar (sometimes transliterated as "Koch Bihar"). Through vacillating, tenuous victories each side's forces would often find themselves occupying perforated tracts of territory that contained within them isolated landlords (and perhaps stubborn chieftains and disbanded soldiers) still loyal to the other side. By 1713, both sides seemed to have grown weary of the back-and-forth and so they reached a fixed settlement of which power would control which tracts of land in the region. The agreement simply cemented the status quo, allowing the lands presently held by or loyal to either the Mughals or the Kingdom of Cooch Behar to remain the sovereign territory of that respective power. Though this arrangement meant that some of each power's lands were disconnected from their own principal territory (and surrounded by the territory of a former enemy), it posed no significant problem to regional administration given the power's feudal nature and the conventions of territorial administration at the time (Chaki, 2011; Edward, 2013; Jones, 2009; van Schendel, 2002; Vinokurov, 2007; Whyte, 2002).

The British East India Company wrested effective control over the Mughal territories in the Bengal region in the mid-eighteenth century, lands which then came under direct control of the British Crown with the 1858 Government of India Act (Harrington, 2010; Metcalf & Metcalf, 2012; O'Ballance, 1957; van Schendel, 2002; Whyte, 2002). Though the British also captured Cooch Behar a couple of decades later, they allowed the Maharaja there to continue to administer his own lands as a princely state—under the ultimate suzerainty of the British, of course. The year 1713's on-the-ground jurisdictional differences thus remained; the former Mughal lands of Bengal, including its exclaves, were under direct British rule, while the princely state of Cooch Behar and its retained exclaves were at least nominally ruled by the local Maharaja (Bartholomew, 1893, p. 92; van Schendel, 2002; Whyte, 2002).

Whyte (2002, p. 40) finds that the British not only did not create the enclaves on the frontier of British India, but were apparently unaware for some time that they even existed. He cites an 1814 letter from the Acting Magistrate of Rangpur which reads in part:

> "I found patches (if I may be allowed the expression) of territory, which, though surrounded by such parts of the Cooch Behar Rajah's Estate, as pay revenue to Government, have, by some unaccountable accident, been long held independent of the Honourable Company ... Not even in these isolated spots has the Magistrate's authority ever been exerted, either in the way of general superintendence, or even on occasion, when public offenders may have evaded the pursuit of the Police, by openly taking refuge in such assylums [sic]."

Attempts were made by the British to exchange the enclaves (which were then between the princely state of Cooch Behar and the Rangpur division of British India) in the early twentieth century, as the British recognised early on that they were an impediment to the efficient administration of the region (Jones, 2009; Whyte, 2002). None of those attempts were successful, however, in part because of local opposition. The Enclaves' boundaries, along with the rest of the Cooch Behar-Rangpur dividing line, were thus surveyed and demarcated with markers in the 1930s (Hartley, 1940; Whyte, 2002).

Just before the British were to leave the Subcontinent in mid-1947, the aforementioned barrister Radcliffe was brought from Europe to draw up lines partitioning British India into an independent Indian republic and the new state of Pakistan. British India did not include Cooch Behar, however, so the existing boundaries of the princely state were not addressed by Radcliffe or his Boundary Commission. Rather, the Maharaja of Cooch Behar was given the choice for his lands—including its exclaves then within the Rangpur division—to either become part of India or part of Pakistan (Whyte, 2002).

Two years after India's independence, Maharaja Jagaddipendra Narayan personally chose the former. In his 2011 book, Chaki includes a copy of the contract (pp. 136-40) termed the "Cooch Behar Merger Agreement," which details the provisions by which the princely state of Cooch Behar would become part of India. The contract shows that much attention was given to ensuring the continued comfort of Narayan after the handover of his lands to India, including an annual tax-free stipend of 850,000 rupees for the rest of his life, as well as other provisions for his family after his own passing. The Maharaja was also guaranteed personal guards, a children's marital trust fund, fixed-rate electricity at his home, and free water utility services.

Less attention seems to have been paid to the effects Narayan's agreement with the Indian government would have for his former subjects. For two years some of Narayan's lands had already been surrounded by the sovereign territory of the independent state of Pakistan (and there were then of course Pakistani pockets of land by then within his realm, too). His choice for these lands to go to India instead of surrounding Pakistan thus made the boundaries around the area's enclaves truly international for the first time in their roughly 250-year history (Chaki, 2011; van Schendel, 2002; Whyte, 2002). Yet research for this paper did not uncover any evidence that the many difficulties sure to come with the internationalising of nearly 200 enclaves was considered by Narayan before he signed the agreement. Nonetheless in a farewell message to his people before leaving his Cooch Behar palace, Narayan promised:

> "We shall always watch with keen interest your moral and material welfare and always pray for your happiness and prosperity." (Chaki, 2011, p. 142)

The enclaves of Central Asia (however many there may be) cannot rightly be connected with the hands of Joseph Stalin. But they often are, nonetheless. In a June 2010 article titled "Stalin's harvest," the *Economist* outlined the history of Central Asia's complex boundaries (p. 28):

> "In 1924 Stalin divided the region into different Soviet republics. The borders were drawn up rather arbitrarily without following strict ethnic lines or even the guidelines of topography. The main aim was to counter the growing popularity of pan-Turkism in the region and to avoid potential friction ... Some of the borders were redrawn several times until 1936. After 1991, this lead to lively demarcation disputes among the newly independent countries. In addition, some small pockets of territory are nominally part of one country but geographically isolated from it. Kyrgyzstan, for example, has seven enclaves, two belonging to Tajikistan and five to Uzbekistan."

In a separate article of the same issue (this one titled "Stalin's latest victims") the *Economist* says dramatically (p. 15):

> "Faced with the difficulty of ruling a region as tumultuous as Central Asia, Stalin divided it into a patchwork of states whose borders were designed to fracture races and smash nationalism."

Kaiser and Raimondo (2002) similarly explain the origin of the Central Asian boundaries this way:

> "Uncle Joe Stalin gets the credit. After the Bolsheviks defeated the last of the Central Asian rebels, more than a decade after their 1917 revolution, they decided to organise Central Asia into five republics. Stalin helped draw the borders. They were apparently intended to discourage any idea that these jurisdictions could ever be independent countries."

Whatever the track record of Joseph Stalin, the enclaves of the region and the chaos they are now causing are not quite his fault. Moreover, the boundaries of Central Asia's enclaves never caused any real concern when they were originally established, as with those in South Asia. It was their internationalisation—their acceptance and fixing, either intentionally or as the surely foreseeable result of other actions, as the boundaries of newly independent states—by others later on which in fact made them so problematic.

Contrary to those quoted above, Maynes (2003) suggests that the boundaries splitting up Central Asia were created solely on the basis of nationality as part of an effort under Soviet nationality policy to keep like-ethnolinguistic groups together within the same Soviet republic. He says that because there were pockets of Uzbeks, Tajiks, and Kyrgyz irregularly scattered throughout Central Asia, this sometimes led to the creation of enclaves. A village of Uzbeks, for example, was made part of the Uzbek Soviet Socialist Republic even if it was surrounded by a population of ethnic Krygyz, in order to keep members of the same ethnolinguistic group together. But he also explains that this patchwork geography did not much matter in Soviet times because the Soviet Union's internal borders "were only symbolic" (p. 127) and not affecting the day-to-day lives of the region's inhabitants.

Maynes is correct in this second point. The boundaries between Central Asia's Soviet republics were never intended to be international ones and posed no restriction to the free movement of goods and people across them. In fact, the extensive infrastructure network built by the Soviets seems to have encouraged cross-border movement, the region's busy roads, rails, and pipelines weaving about the intra-republic boundaries as if they did not exist at all (Megoran, 2012).

But, Maynes errs if his larger claim is that the boundaries of Central Asia, including those around the enclaves, are purely the outcomes of Soviet policies to bring members of defined nationalities into the same administrative unit (whether that unit was geographically contiguous or not). That Central Asia's enclaves are not based on nationality is obvious by the fact that some Soviet republics' (now independent states') enclaves were and still are largely populated by the ethnic nationals of a neighbour. Indeed while Maynes says the large enclave of Sokh is "Uzbek-populated" (p. 127), this sovereign territory of Uzbekistan within Kyrgyzstan is, actually, almost entirely comprised of ethnic Tajiks (International Crisis Group, 2002; IRIN News Service, 2001; Myrzabekova & Sikorskaya, 2013; Radio Free Europe/Radio Liberty, 2013; Trilling, 2013). In other words Sokh is a community of Tajiks surrounded by Kyrgyz peoples, but its territory is neither part of Tajikistan or Kyrgyzstan; it is part of Uzbekistan and its people are Uzbek citizens. This is not minor detail, either. It is a fact essential to understanding the current foreign policy challenges—and opportunities—of the region, as will become clear in following sections of this paper.

So was the *Economist*, as well as Kaiser and Raimondo (2002), right after all? Did Stalin purposefully divide and tie up nationalities in Central Asia just to make things difficult for the people that lived there? Hirsch (2000) does not think so. In fact as she points out, this would have been against the Soviet Union's presumed interests of regional stability and prosperity. Soviet bureaucratic planners (the ones who really drew the boundaries) spent a great deal of effort working to ensure peace among local populations by drawing "administratively viable national-territorial units" (p. 218). This, as Hirsch explains, meant considering ethno-national, as well as economic and logistical factors when determining which lands should go to which republic.

Central Asia's enclaves are the product of such efforts to "balance" the republics, and therefore bring stability. Dadabaev (2012), Megoran (2012), and Nuttall (2013) explain that the Central Asian Soviet republics were permitted to swap territories with one another as they needed so as to achieve what they recognised was possible. If one of the republics needed more lands for agriculture or for better access to scarce water resources, they could simply buy or lease tracts of territory from a neighbour. After all, each was part of the larger Soviet Union, the boundaries of bought or leased lands did not affect the local population, and uniform prosperity was the ultimate goal. It thus could be said that the region's enclaves were originally intended to make life easier for its people.

As with the enclaves in South Asia, Central Asia's enclaves did not become a problem until they were associated with fully independent states (Dadabaev, 2012). Like the Maharaja of Cooch Behar choosing for his lands to become Indian without considering how its enclaves and exclaves would function, revolutionaries of early-1990s Central Asia sought and gained independence for Kyrgyzstan, Tajikistan, and Uzbekistan without first cleaning up the boundaries between each other. Their enclaves were at most an afterthought.

It is reasonable to question whether the history of how the enclaves were created really matters. This paper argues that it does, particularly to those who design political geographies and to those whose lives their creations affect. The problem with repeating ahistorical accounts of how the enclaves were made is that it stymies critical reflection into how our world's political geographies are created and perpetuated. Through the fog of these myths, we cannot see how the distracted choices to commit to certain seemingly harmless boundaries now can have troublesome consequences later. Even today, there are countries drawing subnational enclaves with domestic administrative boundaries,[6] presumably thinking like the early Maharajas, Mughal princes, and Soviet land leasers that the functions of their boundaries will always stay the same.

Behind these myths, we also miss opportunities to hold our more contemporary native leadership to account for the boundaries they in fact gave us, instead casting blame on foreign figures of yesteryear or just unfortunate happenstance. In a way, boundary myths help to perpetuate the feeling that we are helpless, that we are only passive victims born into an inescapable cage of lines from history, rather than active agents fully capable of simply drawing a more rational map.

And surely a new map is needed if critical policy goals are to be achieved and national commitments fulfilled. The very existence of the enclaves in South and Central Asia undermines efforts of states in these regions to foster economic development, reduce crime, mitigate threats to regional security, support democratic institutions, grow healthy communities, and live up to their own stated ideals of human equality. The connection between the complex political geography of two states, India and Kyrgyzstan, and the success of some of their most important public policies is considered further in the following section.

6. For example, the Alaskan native village of Klukwan is not included in the municipality of Haines Borough completely surrounding it, leaving Klukwan a subnational enclave (Division of Community and Regional Affairs, 2012).

CHAPTER FOUR

Enclave Effects On Policy Goals

The effects of enclaves are a function of how these geographic features actually manifest themselves in physical space. The enclaves of South and Central Asia are useful case studies for demonstrating this principal because they quite literally look so different on the ground, and thus lead to contrasting conditions for their inhabitants and their governments' policies.

With the only exception of Dahagram-Angarpota,[7] the boundaries of the South Asian enclaves are invisible. There are no fences or signs marking these enclaves' edges, no manned checkpoints guarding their entrances. With enough searching one may be able to spot the occasional boundary post ("BP") audaciously delaminating either country's claim, but these markers, originally installed during the British era (Whyte, 2002), are reportedly being removed by local villagers and are otherwise typically covered in overgrown brush. Indeed, one can pass into, through, and out of the South Asian enclaves without even knowing it, these sovereign pieces of territory blending in with their surrounding farmland entirely. Critical to understanding the effects of the South Asian enclaves is that their boundaries really only exist on paper and in the lives of area residents.

Now as one might expect, given the degree of disagreement on other details, the actual number of residents in the South Asian enclaves is also disputed. Many sources, including Ghosh (2013), Sattar (2012), and Pandey (2011) say the population of both the Indian and Bangladeshi

7. All further references to the enclaves of South Asia in this paper will except Dahagram-Angarpota because it is the only enclave of the 198 shared between India and Bangladesh that is fenced and permanently guarded, its residents afforded services and official identification, and, as will be noted later, is not under consideration for transfer to its surrounding state.

enclaves totals somewhere between 50,000 and 70,000 people. These estimates are roughly in line with the first and only official joint government census of the enclaves taken back in 2011 (Bose, 2011; Sengupta, 2013), which found there to be about 51,000 people. However, Jones (2009), Rahman, Murshed, and Sultana (2013) say there could actually be as many as 100,000 people. Harun ur Rashid (2011), a former ambassador of Bangladesh to the United Nations, claims there are between 100,000 and 200,000 residents of South Asia's enclaves.

However many there may really be, these lives are shaped not by their physical containment (again, 197 enclaves have no fences), but rather by their de facto statelessness. The problems faced by the enclave residents and, as this paper argues, by their states, stem from the fact that these people lack any official identification and are not afforded any government services (Ghosh, 2013; Jones, 2009; Sattar, 2012; van Schendel, 2002). These two conditions are in fact related to each other and themselves the outcomes of stubborn notions of a state's territorial sovereignty in an area of such complex political geography.

Van Schendel (2002, p. 124) aptly describes the situation as "kafka-esque." See, because there are no government offices in the South Asia enclaves, residents do not have local access to the appropriate agencies that issue identification documents. Yet they cannot travel to other government offices in their country's principal territory to obtain the identification documents either, as such travel would mean crossing international territory—which requires official identification, such as passports and visas (Jones, 2009; van Schendel, 2002; Whyte, 2002). In other words, enclave residents cannot obtain official identification because they do not already have official identification.

It is this lack of recognised identification combined with the lack of government services locally that renders South Asia's enclave residents so vulnerable. This paper further argues that such vulnerability of enclave residents harms the interests and commitments of their respective states. Given space constraints and that Bangladesh has already formally acted to dissolve the enclaves with its unilateral ratification of the 1974 Land

Boundary Agreement, this paper chooses to specifically address the effects of South Asia's enclaves on the interests and commitments of India. Note, however, that the living conditions and circumstances of those in Bangladesh's exclaves in India are analogous to those of residents of India's exclaves within Bangladesh.

India's Department of Border Management (2012, pp. 1-2) says that among its "principal objectives" is to secure India's international borders against "interests hostile to the country," while facilitating "legitimate trade and commerce" with neighbouring countries. Presumably recognising that true border security necessitates the socio-economic well-being of people and communities along them—as Espach and Haering (2012) have in analysing the management of Central America's borders and Dessì (2012) has while examining conditions of Egypt's Sinai—the Department implements the Border Area Development Programme (BADP). Through a "comprehensive approach" BADP aims to "meet the special developmental needs of the people living in remote and inaccessible areas" along India's international borders and to "promote a sense of security and well-being among the border population" (Ministry of Home Affairs, 2012, p. 24). BADP does this by providing funding for the construction of basic infrastructure, such as roads, schools, water utilities, and electrical and telephone facilities, in border communities to foster their sustainable development and in the end, the security of India. West Bengal, the state to which India's exclaves belong and within which Bangladesh's exclaves are located, received 25 crore rupees (approximately 5 million US dollars) in funds from the national government for BADP projects between the years of 2006 and 2010 (Ministry of Home Affairs, 2012).

None of these funds have been spent on projects in India's exclaves, ostensibly because government agencies cannot reach them (Datta, 2011). This goes back to the earlier point about the exercise of territorial sovereignty in enclave geography. With the exception of the 2011 census, the governments of India and Bangladesh have always, at least formally, prohibited neighbouring officials and administrative agents, be they border guards, police officers, politicians, or public works contractors, from crossing their sovereign territory so that neighbours may access its enclaves.

The *de jure* Indian citizens who reside in these pockets thus continue to be without the most basic of human necessities. This has been widely reported for years. What has not been stressed, though, is how such deplorable conditions undermine the Department of Border Management's efforts to develop border communities, promote a sense security among their people, and thus protect the Indian homeland, or how the lack of critical infrastructure and services in these Indian territories runs contrary to other government goals and commitments.

For example, the Department of School Education and Literacy (2012) reminds that, according to the Constitution of India, all children in the country have the right to free and compulsory elementary education.

The government promises to provide the school buildings and the teachers. The Department states emphatically that universal elementary education is necessary for "strengthening the social fabric of democracy" and that the Department is working toward universal access and retention and the "bridging of gender and social category gaps" through education (Department of School Education and Literacy, 2013). The Ministry of Human Resource Development (2012) says further:

> "The essence of Human Resource Development is education, which plays a significant and remedial role in balancing the socio-economic fabric of the Country. Since citizens of India are its most valuable resource, our billion-strong nation needs the nurture and care in the form of basic education to achieve a better quality of life."

Yet, Indian children have no access to education if they happen to live in one of their country's exclaves. There are no schools within the exclaves and their children cannot attend any other schools nearby because they do not possess—and, as noted earlier, cannot obtain—the required identification documents permitting their enrolment (BBC News, 2013; Institute of Foreign Policy Studies, 2012; Jones, 2009; Pandey, 2011; *The Daily Star*, 2012; Whyte, 2002). Under the current circumstances of political geography, the Government of India's efforts and promises to provide universal elementary education cannot be fully achieved.

What is more, because thousands of exclave children lack even a basic education, they grow up only able to find the most remedial work, such as pulling rickshaws in nearby towns or tobacco, jute, or vegetable farming (Sarkar D., 2012; Sengupta, 2013). This labour might only earn them 100 or 200 rupees (just one or two US dollars) each day—hardly enough to support the needs of a family (Sengupta, 2013). The exclaves thus can be said to undermine the Indian government's hopes to reduce poverty, increase domestic consumer spending, and improve individuals' quality of life with the growth of advantageous employment opportunities, goals described by the Department of Industrial Policy and Promotion (2008) and generalised by Lewis (2012). In its strategic action plan, India's Department of Commerce cites low literacy levels and the poor quality of technical education as "weaknesses" (2012, pp. 2-3) inhibiting its efforts to grow the country's exports and promote trade. The enclaves, by preventing tens of thousands of people from receiving basic education, surely exacerbate these weaknesses and deny India its full economic potential.

India's health policies are also jeopardised by the enclaves. The Department of Health and Family Welfare's (DHFW's) stated vision for 2013-2104 is to ensure:

> "availability of quality healthcare on equitable, accessible and affordable basis [sic] across regions and communities with special focus [sic] on under-served population [sic] and marginalised groups" (2013, p. 3).

DHFW has enumerated several objectives in line with this policy, including the provision of universal access to primary health care services, the improvement of maternal and child health, and a reduction in the "disease burden" on Indian society (p. 3). There are no medical facilities of any kind in India's exclaves, however, and, as with area schools, exclave residents cannot access hospitals nearby because they have no official identification (BBC News, 2013; Institute of Foreign Policy Studies, 2012; Jones, 2009; Pandey, 2011; *The Daily Star*, 2012; Whyte, 2002). Without any medical care, exclave residents often die of otherwise curable diseases, such as cholera (Jones, 2009, p. 373).

Adding to the exclaves' health challenges is the fact they have no proper infrastructure for the provision of clean, safe drinking water either (Pandey, 2011; Rashid, 2011; van Schendel, 2002; WaterAid, 2011). This is despite contemporary judicial interpretations that the right to safe drinking water is guaranteed by the Constitution of India (Kothari, 2006; Upadhyay, 2011). It is also despite the Government of West Bengal's explicit aim to grow the state "by minimising spatial imbalance and rural push [sic] through intensive adoption of rural water supply and sanitation programmes" (Public Health and Engineering Department, 2012) and the identification of water quality standards by the state's Public Health and Engineering Department (Public Health and Engineering Department, 2012).

To be sure, the state has implemented a formal, protective West Bengal State Water Policy. The policy begins by stating, "water is the basic need for the existence of all living things in the world. It is the prime natural resource useful for the development of the [sic] human beings" (Government of West Bengal, 2011, p. 1). The water policy includes commitments by the state to explore all sources of water "to the fullest extent" (p. 4), providing drinking water "to the entire population both in urban and rural areas" (p. 5) as the highest priority in any development project, and promising in no uncertain terms that "drinking water and domestic needs of the total population of West Bengal is to be fully made by the year 2025" (p. 6). But, West Bengal's water policy cannot be fully implemented under current circumstances of political geography.

Visits to several Indian exclaves in May 2013 revealed that

improvised, rudimentary electrical connections to occasional structures could be made with generators. However, there are no fixed, reliable electrical connections to India's exclaves (Jones, 2009) and so the residents by and large rely on candles for lighting (BBC, 2013). Similarly, there are no gas, telephone, or internet utility connections from either the Indian or Bangladeshi mainlands to the territories. West Bengal's Department of Power nonetheless explains that it is working to promote the state's economic growth with efforts directed to rural areas, as it makes clear in this statement (Department of Power and Non-Conventional Energy Sources, n.d.):

> "The stress, now, is on the commensurate strengthening of the transmission and distribution network in the state to widely disperse the availability of quality power specially [sic] in rural Bengal."

It is the established and well-publicised goal of the government of West Bengal to have one of the leading information technology industries among the states of India. The state's "Policy on Information and Communication Technology, 2012" explicitly identifies the need to connect its rural population with information technology (IT) and information technology-enabled services (ITeS) activities in order to achieve that larger vision. While "recognising the importance of e-literacy in overall development of the child" (p. 3) the policy also promises that all West Bengal children will be given exposure to basic computer skills in elementary school, and further commits that by 2017 "every family in the State has at least one e-literate member amongst it" (p. 4). With such improvements in its communication infrastructure and e-knowledge base, West Bengal believes it will be able to enhance the availability of skilled manpower, better attract business investors, and even improve government efficiency and accountability (Department of Information Technologies and Electronics, 2012). It is not clear, though, how the Government of West Bengal plans to meet the inclusive commitments of its IT/ITeS growth policy without being able to reach its citizens in its exclaves. It therefore will likely have tens of thousands of unskilled youth unable to contribute to the state's IT/ITeS-centred economic development, and not able to help improve government accountability and efficiency.

Perhaps the most critical deficiency in India's exclaves is the absence of law enforcement. There are no police stations, public safety officials, or security agents of any kind in any of India's 106 exclaves (BBC News, 2013; Jones, 2009; Whyte, 2002). Indeed, the country's law enforcement personnel are not even able to access their exclaves from India's principal territory as this would violate agreements with Bangladesh prohibiting their transit across even the thinnest portions of sovereign Bangladeshi lands. Such restrictive circumstances no doubt frustrate the stated aims and objectives of the West Bengal Police, which are to "prevent and detect crime, and bring to justice those who break the law" by applying the law "fairly and firmly." The police "strive to keep the State peaceful" and "to protect people through active cooperation of the community" (West Bengal Police, n.d.), but these commitments are not and cannot be met in these isolated lands.

Security commitments at the national level are also compromised. Officially, India's Narcotics Control Bureau (NCB) is tasked with enforcing a number of policies to curb the trafficking of contraband substances into the country. Land border surveillance and enforcement, interdiction along "known drug routes," and "identification and eradication of illicit cultivation" of drugs such as cannabis are cited as some of the Bureau's primary counter-narcotics efforts (Narcotics Control Bureau, 2013). Yet it is not possible for the NCB to implement these policies in the exclaves given current sensitivities toward territorial sovereignty and integrity shared between India and Bangladesh (*Deccan Herald*, 2013; Gupta S., 2011; Habib, 2003) which, again, preclude foreign security forces from transiting across each other's lands.

So without any on-site protection by state- or national-level law enforcement, the residents are left to defend themselves against criminals who exploit the enclave geography to the detriment of personal, regional, and national security. Many have described how India's exclaves have been turned into bases for drug and human trafficking in consequence. The traffickers use the territories as safe havens of operation because they know they cannot be reached in them by any country's law enforcement and because they are close to the principal boundary between India and Bangladesh with better access to large consumer markets. The exclaves have also been used for the very cultivation of illicit drugs, with cannabis farming in the exclaves sometimes cited as an important (and of course illegal) source of enclave residents' income.

Biswas (2000) argues the exclaves could also be exploited by nearby militant extremist groups to launch attacks against mainland India. Others who share such national security fears believe extremist groups, of which there are several active already in the region (Ahmed, 2009; Baruah, 2009; Biswas, 2000; Zaman, 2012), could use the exclaves' isolation and lack of law enforcement, and draw on the rising sense of hopelessness and disaffection among their residents.[8]

It is important to consider that the enclaves may also have particularly adverse effects on the condition of women despite concerted policies to empower women and promote gender equality. Drawing on the history of the Dahagram-Angarpota enclave before the establishment of the Tin Bigha Corridor, Cons (2012, p. 546) explains how enclave conditions trapped female residents in without access to medical care, and thus women commonly died of complications related to childbirth. He also details a history of men from neighbouring villages kidnapping, raping, and torturing vulnerable enclave women. Whyte (2002, p. 184) further explains how the enclaves make marriages for local residents difficult, both because of their disconnection and because their lack of official identification makes them less suitable spouses. On a visit to Indian enclaves in Bangladesh in 2013, villagers reported to

8. It should be noted though that others, while agreeing that there are the seeds for violent extremist organisations in Bangladesh or Assam state, believe there is little threat of extremist cells being established in and operating from the South Asian enclaves. Sengupta (2013) is one of those who discounts the extremist potentiality, noting that the enclave residents are "so peaceful and honest" (p. 3) in their daily lives.

this author that enclave geography affects the female residents' marriage opportunities more than local males. As they explained, women from "outside" (who generally had official identification) would relocate to the enclave in order to marry and live with a man. Conversely, women from within the enclave, because they lacked official identification, typically found it difficult to find a husband. Unmarried women in more traditional parts South Asia may be at a socio-economic disadvantage, for various reasons (Asia Society, 2011; Centre for Study of Society and Secularism, 2011).

Kishor and Gupta (2009, p. 4) highlight that India is a signatory to the United Nations Millennium Development Goals (MDGs), which seek a reduction in maternal mortality, the promotion of gender equity, and the overall empowerment of women at all levels of society (United Nations, 2013). India's Ministry of Women and Child Development has had since 2001 an adopted "National Policy for the Empowerment of Women," which enumerates specific provisions to achieve a broad range of stated objectives, including:

- The elimination of discrimination and all forms of violence against women
- Equal access to women to health care and social security
- Equal access to participation and decision-making of women in social, political, and economic life of the nation
- De jure and de facto enjoyment of all human rights and fundamental freedom by women on equal basis with men in all spheres

The gender imbalances created by the enclaves as described in this paper surely run contrary to these policy goals and commitments.

It is clear then that a broad range of fundamental domestic policy priorities of both the national government of India and the government of West Bengal State—from public safety and national security, to education, economic development, basic healthcare, and gender equality—cannot be fully achieved because of, and perhaps are even set back by, India's exclaves. More precisely, it is India's understanding that it cannot cross Bangladeshi territory to service its exclaves which hinders these efforts, as well as the enclave residents' inability to obtain official identification. One seemingly obvious remedy to this situation arises: India and Bangladesh committing to some reciprocal agreement whereby each country permits sufficient transit rights to the other so that it may access its exclaves, and provide necessary services.

Yet it is highly unlikely any such agreement would ever materialise. Partly this is because of the current and historic quality of relations between the two countries, which are characterised by Barbhuiya (2009) and Zia (2012), as well as five decades of precedent regarding territorial sovereignty. Further, both countries have already stated intentions to transfer enclave territory, so any efforts toward actually connecting the isolated territories to their homelands with infrastructure and services would be cast as pointless (there would be no need to provide expensive utility connections to the exclaves or build schools in them if they are going to be given to a neighbour soon anyway). Even if it were to connect the exclaves now, the logistical challenges of planning, operating, administering, and maintaining so many services and infrastructures across complex international boundaries would be profoundly complicated, surely inefficient, and likely unsustainable. The fulfilment of the aforementioned domestic policies and commitments thus seem helplessly constrained by intractable, impenetrable enclave geography.

But so are India's foreign policies. Barbhuyia (2009, p. 44) talks about how the enclave issue "continues to be an irritant in Indo-Bangladesh bilateral relations." Bangladesh has for decades awaited and urged India's ratification of the draft agreement to dissolve their shared enclaves, which, again, is known as the "Land Boundary Agreement" (LBA), thus ending the tragic circumstances which comprise Bangladesh's own domestic policy goals and trap thousands of its own citizens. Implementation of the LBA is also attractive to Bangladesh because it would mean a net gain of about 10,000 acres of territory. Bangladesh formally ratified the agreement back in 1974, but India, despite repeated promises as late as this year, has not done so (Whyte, 2002). Solving the "enclaves issue" by ratifying and implementing the LBA could help breed trust and goodwill among the two countries and facilitate efforts to address other contentious issues between them, including illegal migration and water sharing.

Poplin (2013) argues that better relations between Delhi and Dhaka could lead to more cross-border investment. This would result in the growth of Bangladesh's economy, which is in India's own economic interests. Gupta (2011, p. 2) also encourages India to improve relations with its neighbours, including Bangladesh, in part to counterbalance the growing influence of China in South Asia.

While perhaps not their primary issue of mutual concern, Bangladeshi voters certainly hope to see the resolution of the enclaves issue with India as they foresee some of these perceived benefits to their country as well. In fact, the Aspen Institute of India (n.d.) explains that the continued existence of the enclaves remains a political problem for an Awami League often portrayed by opposition parties as too supportive of neighbouring India. So while India might see a net loss of territory with the dissolution of the enclaves, resolution of the decades-old dispute will help to support the Awami League in upcoming elections—and the Awami League is surely better for the interests of India than the likely opposition. This is just the argument made by the *Times of India* in April 2013 when it urged:

> "A friendly Awami League-led dispensation in Dhaka has helped New Delhi address its security concerns by moving against anti-Indian insurgents operating from its soil. With general elections in Bangladesh slated to be announced by the end of the year, India's failure to come good on the LBA and the Teesta accord would strengthen the hand of India baiters in that country. Seen in the context of the US withdrawal from Afghanistan, New Delhi can ill afford to have inimical forces gain advantage in Dhaka."

The costs of India's exclaves are plainly stark and wide-ranging. Their continued existence breeds insecurity, inhibits economic growth, causes social and even physical harm, and disrupts strategic relations with its neighbour Bangladesh. And India seems to recognise these costs, at least rhetorically. The country has acknowledged the benefits of dissolving the enclaves through statements and draft agreements since the 1950s which this paper will review in Section Five. Though, as that final section will also show, various forces in India have consciously worked to preserve the enclaves at the same time. What these forces believe they can gain from preserving the enclaves must be truly compelling.

Enclaves in Central Asia also undermine the interests and stated policy goals of Kyrgyzstan, but such "policy jeopardy" is brought about by different circumstances and characteristics than the enclaves in South Asia, including differences in their administration, their spatial distribution, and their physical manifestation. For instance, residents of the South Asian enclaves are not prevented by physical barriers or border checkpoints from exiting their land to buy and sell simple goods or take basic jobs; so long as they go formally undetected by local authorities (or pay those authorities the occasional bribe), they are able to enter the surrounding foreign territory. Sengupta (2013) reports that there is even a kind of gentlemen's agreement in Dinhata, India, whereby local authorities tacitly permit the residents of nearby enclaves and counter-enclaves to come into town as they need (though they are still of course not able to access schools, hospitals, and other public facilities because they are technically illegal immigrants without identification documents). This is largely not the case in Kyrgyzstan's several enclaves, or in its exclave village of Barak. The movement of people into and out of these territories is much more constrained and enclave society is more segregated from that of the surrounding country.

The results of such differences in levels of enclave isolation are illustrated by the varied economic habits of their residents. In the enclaves of South Asia residents use the same currency of the surrounding state; those in exclaves of Bangladesh use Indian rupees and residents of India's exclaves use Bangladeshi taka, as any commerce largely takes place in the communities outside of the enclaves (Sengupta, 2013; Whyte, 2002).

Conversely, residents of Central Asian enclaves tend to use the currency of their "home state" and abide by its time zone, which can differ from that of the surrounding "host" (Maynes, 2003; Megoran, 2012). The residents of Central Asian enclaves generally do not—and cannot—leave to engage in commerce in the immediately-surrounding territory, as enclave residents in South Asia do routinely.

This is largely because the boundaries of the Central Asian enclaves are far less permeable than those in South Asia. Stricter border controls along the edges of Central Asia's enclaves are the result of more than a decade of conspicuous mistrust that has occasionally morphed into violent conflict among the Central Asian states since their independence from the Soviet Union, with the Uzbek-Kyrgyz relationship being particularly acrid.

Though the Central Asian states originally had a symbiotic relationship with each other as Soviet republics, Megoran (2012) explains how their economies began to drift apart just after independence, in the meantime adopting different currencies, different writing scripts, and even different rules for the practice of daylight savings. The real divergence in Uzbek-Kyrgyz relations, though, and real trouble for their enclaves' residents, came in 1999 after Uzbek authorities blamed foreign religious extremists for a terrorist attack in their country's capital, Tashkent. Believing the perpetrators at the very least transited through Kyrgyzstan, the Uzbeks temporarily sealed the Uzbek-Kyrgyz border. They were only partially reopened later that year—and with a much greater security presence and with heightened conceptions of competing nationalisms on both sides (Cohen, 2004; Maynes, 2003; Megoran, 2012; Polat & Butkevich, 2000).

It is for those estimated 40,000-55,000[9] people living in the several Uzbek territories inside of Kyrgyzstan (International Crisis Group, 2002; Turgayev, 2013; Vinokurov, 2007) and the 600-1,200[10] people

9. Most sources place the population of Sokh, together with the other Uzbek enclaves in the Kyrgyz Republic, as somewhere in this range. However, Myrzabekova and Sikorskaya (2013) recently reported that the population of Sokh alone has "risen to almost 70,000."

10. The International Crisis Group (2002) did not estimate the population of Barak, but rather stated that it had 627 households (p. 15).

living in the single Kyrgyz exclave inside of Uzbekistan (AKIpress News Agency, 2013; Kimsanov, 2003; Vinokurov, 2007) that international conflict and resulting border closures have had their sharpest impact. Yet, these enclaves also continue to harm the domestic and international policy interests of broader Kyrgyzstan.

Barak, the sovereign Kyrgyz territory just 1.5 kilometres from the main Uzbek-Kyrgyz boundary (Radio Free Europe/Radio Liberty, 2011), exemplifies the former circumstance. The village-sized exclave has no high school and no proper medical facilities (International Crisis Group, 2002), so residents must transit across Uzbek territory to the nearby city of Osh in Kyrgyzstan's principal territory for these services. According to a village leader interviewed by the United Nation's IRIN News Service (2005), residents of Barak largely rely on income generated from exporting cotton grown in the exclave and import most other basic goods on visits to the Kyrgyz mainland. Barak families are also divided by geography. Some members live in the exclave and others in the principal territory of the Kyrgyz Republic (Radio Free Europe/Radio Liberty, 2011; Niyazova, 2013).

Crossing foreign territory to go to school or to the hospital, to sell and buy necessities, and to visit relatives is not an otherwise unheard-of lifestyle. That residents of the USA's Hyder and Point Roberts and the Netherlands' Baarle-Nassau also have to transit through a sovereign neighbour to access the closest schools, hospitals, and other basic services, or to simply go shopping, shows that similar situations exist in other parts of the globe (Berg, 2012; Division of Community and Regional Affairs, 2012; Gelbman & Timothy, 2011). What is unusual and so problematic about Barak's geographical situation is that the Uzbeks make it so difficult for its villagers to leave. Generally citing security concerns or the need to retaliate for alleged smuggling along other sections of their border with the Kyrgyz Republic, the Uzbeks will routinely limit the amount of goods Barak residents can take across its territory and the frequency of their travel. Villagers have long reported being harassed by Uzbek border guards and unnecessarily delayed, which adds to their transport costs—if they are allowed to cross at all (International Crisis Group, 2002; IRIN News Service, 2005; Radio Free Europe/Radio Liberty, 2011).

The reasons for the adverse treatment of Kyrgyz nationals by Uzbek border guards may be related to violence targeted at ethnic Uzbeks elsewhere in the Kyrgyz Republic. It is reported that three years ago, a number of villagers from Barak, afraid of reprisals from surrounding Uzbeks for the attacks, managed to flee from the exclave to the Kyrgyz mainland for safety (Fitzpatrick, 2010; Radio Free Europe/Radio Liberty, 2011).

This is an unfortunate and, frankly, avoidable situation for Barak's residents, to be sure. But at least in terms of one's most basic needs, it appears markedly better than the squalid conditions faced by residents of India's exclaves. The residents of Barak do hold official Kyrgyz identification documents (Radio Free Europe/Radio Liberty, 2011) and have at least occasional access to essential goods and services in the mainland. Dudka (2013) recently reported that the village has received dedicated shipments of food supplies and other forms of assistance, apparently from the Kyrgyz government. She also reported that the Kyrgyz government is in talks with their Uzbek counterparts over easing border restrictions for the villagers, though it is not clear how successful those talks will be. The Kyrgyz government has even provided some petitioning Kyrgyz villagers with lands for resettlement in near the city of Osh. Nonetheless, some believe the government will see that some villagers remain in Barak in order to maintain a claim to the territory (Radio Free Europe/Radio Liberty, 2011), a policy decision that will be considered further in the final section of this paper.

Still, though its residents hold official identification and marginally benefit from the demonstrated concern of their national government, Barak does create real inconveniences and tough international tensions that undermine stated policies of Kyrgyzstan. The problems sewn by the largest of Uzbekistan's exclaves within Kyrgyzstan, Sokh, are even deeper. In fact, this is likely the most troublesome chunk of land in all of Central Asia. For Kyrgyzstan, the impact of the Uzbek-owned territory also stems from its inconvenient geographical position and its disputed, but strictly guarded edges.

The only road linking the far south-western reaches of Kyrgyzstan passes right through Sokh (Myrzabekova & Sikorskaya, 2013). Efforts are under way to construct roads around its southern end, but the new, longer transport route will have to pass through difficult mountainous territory. Until then the Kyrgyz lands west of Sokh are effectively exclaves themselves, more or less cut off from the rest of the country. These remote regions are already socio-economically marginalised from the rest of the country and were invaded and temporarily held by the Islamic Movement of Uzbekistan (IMU) in 1999, the same group credited with the attacks in Tashkent earlier that year. Clearly, the Kyrgyz government has every incentive to connect the region, bring it further into Bishkek's orbit, and aid in its development, so as to reduce the prospect of further local dissatisfaction and quell the potential for further security risks (Nuttall, 2013; Passon & Temirkulov, 2004; Polat & Butkevich, 2000; Utyaganova, 2001). Further, the stated national priorities of Kyrgyzstan surely apply to these southwest regions as well, just as they apply to remote Barak.

But, Kyrgyz efforts to connect and develop their country's south-west corner, and fulfil its national policies, have been stymied by regular delays, closures, and blockades of that single road passing through Sokh. The delays may be caused by Uzbek border guards who Khamidov (2008) calls "ill-trained," but, for whatever reason, no doubt harass Kyrgyz commuters or prevent them from passing through at all. The local villagers themselves have held mass protests blocking thru-transit (Passon & Temirkulov, 2004) and earlier this year suddenly closed the enclave's entrances again while taking Kyrgyz nationals then in the enclave hostage (Akhmadov, 2013; Nuttall, 2013).

It is important to consider what motivates these destabilising acts by Sokh residents. Firstly, Sokh is densely populated and therefore land values in the enclave are quite high, as Passon and Temirkulov (2004) explain. Any land disputes (of which there are many, given that the enclave's boundaries are not yet defined) are thus particularly contentious and the obvious conduits of conflict with Sokh's surrounding Kyrgyz villagers. Secondly, the region is arid, but economically dependent on agriculture, so fighting sometimes erupts among locals over scarce water resources. Passon and Temirkulov further explain (p. 24) that "regional cooperation is weak," surely making it difficult for governments to keep otherwise minor disputes from becoming highly disruptive international incidents. In addition to these factors, Akhmadov (2013) feels the communal conflict he describes as an "evolving humanitarian crisis" is exacerbated by an "asymmetrical flow of information" wherein the Kyrgyz media widely reports on conditions, but the Uzbek media largely ignores it. The all-too-familiar dynamics of ethno-national conflict fed by perceived differences in culture, custom, language, and identity are likely at work as well. Yet in whatever degree or formulation, these forces manage to come together to create a tense, antagonistic environment in the area and have triggered numerous transportation disruptions throughout Sokh's short history as an internationalised enclave.

The impacts of severing the road through Sokh, both officially by Uzbek government officials and unofficially by disruptive locals, are not hypothetical, either. Sudden closures in early 2013 required the Kyrgyz government to airlift in food and other essential goods by helicopter to their communities stranded on the opposite side (Nuttall, 2013). But there are other problems for the Kyrgyz Republic created by the enclave other than the opportunity for its aggrieved residents to destabilise the surrounding country with road closures. The construction of a water reservoir within Sokh, for example, forced the partial relocation of the nearby Kyrgyz village of Kara Tokoy. However, because most of the displaced population were from the community's younger generation, Passon and Temirkulov (2004, p. 60) describe how this caused a disintegration of traditional social relations and the "disappearance of social control" among the affected communities. Even this seemingly tangential issue undercuts stated policies of Kyrgyzstan, as will be considered later in this paper.

All this is not to say there have not been some positive developments in enclave conditions over the years. The Uzbeks have reportedly been working to remove the landmines that they laid around their enclaves more than a decade ago, so playing children and grazing farmers can worry a little less about getting blown up if they inadvertently cross the disputed edges of their territory (Dadabaev, 2012; IRIN News Service, 2004; Khamidov, 2009; *The Economist*, 2006). In further positive news for both the residents of the enclave and Kyrgyzstan, Myrzabekova and Sikorskaya have reported that, as of May 2013, the entrances to and out of Sokh are open.

Unfortunately, the remaining strains caused by the existence of enclaves in Central Asia are many. They make the fulfilment of the Kyrgyz Republic's development goals nearly impossible and they continue to complicate and sour critical international relations between the country and neighbouring Uzbekistan, as well as with Tajikistan. In making this argument it is necessary to first examine what the development goals of the Kyrgyz Republic are and how stable relations with Uzbekistan and Tajikistan are in its national interests.

The Government of Kyrgyzstan approved by Decree #239 in 2012 the "Medium Term Development Programme of the Kyrgyz Republic for 2012-2014." The programme outlines a range of specific economic and social development policies the state has committed to pursuing in the coming years. Among these are policies aimed at reducing poverty in rural regions through the growth in agricultural output. Further determining (pp. 21-22) that "tourism is considered as one of key [sic] economic priorities of the country," the programme also lays out specific objectives for the development of the country's latent tourism sector, including an easing of visa requirements, increased advertising of the Kyrgyz Republic overseas, and the "urgent" importance of securing tourists' safety. There are broad aims to ensure access of domestically-produced goods and services to local and regional markets, partly through investments in improved transportation infrastructure, as well as commitments to complete fibre-optic communication lines to Tajikistan and Uzbekistan. Additionally, the programme enumerates initiatives to strengthen the socio-economic conditions of the country with improvements to its education and healthcare systems, and promises to guard Kyrgyzstan's security through the "development of the friendly and mutually beneficial relations with the neighouring countries" (International Monetary Fund, 2012, p. 25).

Subnational units of the country have formalised their own development goals as well. For instance, the Government of Batken Oblast has enumerated extensive plans for the Batken region, the western Kyrgyz territory surrounding Sokh and the other enclaves inside of the country. It hopes to grow the agriculture and tourism industry just as the national government does, as well as mining, food processing, light industry, machine building, and even oil and gas recovery (Government of Batken Oblast, 2010).

It is difficult to see how any of these worthy national and subnational development goals will be fully successful given the logistical disruption and international tension that the enclaves continue to cause. In order to grow the agricultural sector in rural areas, for example, farmers require efficient, reliable transportation infrastructure in order to import supplies such as tractor parts and fertiliser, and to export their product to market. This means more than simply directing resources to build higher quality roads. Indeed such expenses are wasted if those roads can still be closed by foreign border guards or rioting enclave residents. Sudden closures of the only highway through Sokh to western Kyrgyzstan, or the indiscriminate imposition of restrictions on Barak villagers' imports and exports, denies these rural areas' farming industries from being the productive seeds of national development that the Kyrgyz government hopes they will be. The farmers also need easy and predictable access to water resources, but as has been described, these resources are caught up in a mess of disputed political geography that does not conform neatly to the area's environment and makes determining who owns which water reserves difficult and contentious.

Similar difficulties apply to Batken Oblast's goals to develop mining, food processing, and the other export industries just listed. It will be difficult to move these products to market if transportation can be so regularly disrupted by the actions of neighbours in inconveniently-placed enclaves. Tourism growth also requires reliable transportation networks, along with the demonstrated promise of visitors' safety. Both of these preconditions are hindered by the existence of the Central Asian enclaves and therefore render other costly efforts, like the removal of visa requirements or overseas advertising, moot. Similarly, resources directed at branding the Kyrgyz Republic "A Country of Celestial Mountains," as the country's development strategy advocates (p. 22), are no doubt squandered when images of villagers being held hostage in Central Asian enclaves are broadcast around the world.

It was noted earlier how the residents of Barak can only access higher education and medical facilities at the discretion of Uzbek border guards. Because the Kyrgyz government reportedly does not wish for all of these villagers to be relocated to the country's principal territory as noted, and because the challenges of constructing and operating proper education and medical facilities in such a small plot of land stranded inside of a hostile neighbour are not practical, the many hundreds of people in Barak will likely miss out on the stated promises to provide quality education and healthcare services.

Just as they do in South Asia, the continued existence of enclaves in Central Asia limits international cooperation and regional security and prosperity. The ownership, boundaries, administration, and condition of these pieces of land have become a focal point for regional disputes, diverting the attention of the public and their respective governments away from other issues which should be addressed. Always serious and sometimes violent arguments about how to deal with the presence of the enclaves—to work with inherited political geography that may ultimately just be unworkable—likely renders those efforts to establish a regional fibre-optic network, or other efforts to share water and electricity, to create common markets, or to efficiently fight terrorism, all but laudable, lofty dreams.

This section had three main goals. The first was to highlight important differences in the living conditions of South and Central

Asian enclave residents, conditions determined by the nature of their enclaves' administration and their manifestation in physical space. All but one of the enclaves in South Asia are unfenced and not guarded by permanently-stationed agents. This, along with informal agreements in certain areas permitting free local passage, allow the residents of South Asian enclaves to informally transit across at least one international boundary to buy and sell goods, take remedial jobs, and engage with a (legally foreign) community. This cross-border interaction has moulded these residents' sense of national identity with that of the surrounding state. However, residents of South Asian enclaves have not been issued official identification documents, rendering them unable to access schools and hospitals outside of their own territory, unable to vote, and effectively stateless. Conversely, Central Asian enclave residents generally do hold official identification documents, but they are much more restrained in their ability to leave and return to their enclave territory by border security agents—and even landmines.

Despite these differences, this section also hoped to show throughout that there are some similarities in the characteristics of enclaves of South and Central Asia. Their inhabitants lack the same levels of access to critical public services as their mainland counterparts and they are largely reliant on agriculture as a source of income. None of the enclaves in either region are fully self-contained; connections with those outside of the enclaves, be they people in the foreign territory immediately surrounding the enclaves or those in territory further beyond, are important for the social and economic survival.

Finally, this section demonstrated that the very existence of the enclaves in both regions undermines officially stated policies and commitments made by the governments of India and Kyrgyzstan, as well as their assumed interests. Clearly, features of geography have confounded Indian and Kyrgyz efforts to provide education and healthcare, to alleviate poverty, to ensure national security, and to improve regional relations.

But the culprits here are not physical geographic features such as mountains, rivers, and oceans which cannot easily be moved. They are features of political geography which exist only on paper and can be altered with the strokes of a pen. What then remains unanswered is why, given the evidentiary and even acknowledged downsides to such difficult boundaries, the governments who control them just do not draw a better map. The next section of this paper attempts to answer this question.

CHAPTER FIVE

The Enclaves' Continued Existence

Few in India say they like the boundaries the way they are, or that they make any logical sense. In fact, the Indian government has stated repeatedly in the last five decades its desire to redraw the boundaries and exchange enclave territory with both East Pakistan and then independent Bangladesh.

India and Pakistan first drafted an agreement to dissolve the enclaves in the 1950s. This accord is commonly known as the "Nehru-Noon Agreement" for Indian Prime Minister Jawaharlal Nehru and Pakistani Prime Minister Feroz Khan Noon, the countries' respective heads of government at the time. Ratification and implementation of Nehru-Noon stalled, though, after Indian courts ruled that an amendment to the country's constitution was required.[11] Regardless, East Pakistan gained its independence from Pakistan (partly with military assistance by India) and became Bangladesh in 1971,[12] necessitating a new land transfer agreement anyhow (Whyte, 2002).

A new agreement was in fact drafted between India and Bangladesh in 1974, this one typically referred to as the 1974 Land Boundary Agreement (LBA). According to the terms of the LBA, Bangladesh is to gain possession of all Indian exclaves within Bangladesh. India in turn would gain possession of all Bangladeshi exclaves in India—except for the Bangladeshi exclave Dahagram-Angarpota, which would remain sovereign Bangladeshi territory connected through the Tin Bigha

11. India's constitution specifies the country's territorial boundaries, so any boundary change, according to the courts, necessitates an amendment approved by the requisite number of legislators in both houses of Parliament, the Lok Sabha and the Rajya Sabha.
12. Sengupta (2013, p. 2) questions why India did not take Bangladesh's war for independence, in which India assisted, as an opportunity to change its boundary immediately after Bangladesh gained its independence.

Corridor. There is no provision in the LBA for the equitable transfer of acreage in the agreement; rather, as previously noted, it is estimated that India would net a loss of approximately 10,000 acres of territory through the exchange. The Bangladesh parliament ratified the agreement back in 1974. India's has yet to.[13]

But sowing hope, Indian leaders kept promising in the years and decades after Bangladesh's ratification that it will, as well. Then in September 2011, the *Economist* magazine reported on a visit by Indian Prime Minister Manmohan Singh to Bangladesh that year during which he signed another agreement committing to the transfer. Titled "Border agreements: The end of the enclaves," this article triumphantly proclaimed that this signing "marks a watershed" in the two countries' histories by sending the enclaves "to the history books." *The Economist*, as well as some others, was apparently unaware of the legislative process in India and the constitutional amendment requirement for transferring the enclave territory. A largely ceremonial overseas signing by Singh did nothing to change the actual status of the enclaves, just as Nehru was not able to swap the lands on his own without Parliament.

Singh's government does continue to urge Parliament to pass the constitutional amendment and ratification of the Land Boundary Agreement, however. As recently as May 2013, his Minister of External Affairs attempted to introduce the appropriate bill in the Rajya Sabha, but, astoundingly, he was physically prevented from doing so by two members of parliament who rushed the well as soon as the Minister came forward with the bill's paperwork for consideration (*The Hindu*, 2013).

Where does such aggressive opposition come from? Why do some not just ignore the issue, but actively work to stop attempts by others to ratify and implement the LBA? This paper will identify possible reasons for the continued existence of the South Asian enclaves. Some are those expressly stated by members of parliament, state-level politicians, and party members for their own opposition to ratification of the LBA. But

13. For a more comprehensive review of the history of the agreement between India and Pakistan, the Indian court rulings on territorial exchange, and the development of the 1974 LBA, refer to Whyte (2002) and van Schendel (2002).

politicians being politicians, the reasons they give may only be convenient covers for their true motives. Therefore, this paper proposes some other potential explanations as well.

The first possible explanation is a continued sense of "sacred territory." Indeed, the remote enclave lands have been described by some as if they are integral parts of the Indian Homeland just as inseparable as another portion of the country. Promising to soon stand in an Indian exclave and hoist the country's flag, a state spokesman for India's Bharatiya Janata Party (BJP) stated recently in reference to the proposed swap of enclave territory, "We are not going to part with even an inch of our land to Bangladesh" (*The Times of India*, 2013). Of course, such emphatic, uncompromising commitments and symbolic acts of nationalism come despite the somewhat arbitrary nature by which India's exclaves became Indian territory (recall that they became the country's sovereign territory only when the Maharaja of Cooch Behar opted for his princely state to join the then two-year-old republic), and despite the fact that the Government of India has never even administered the territories as it does the rest of its country (Sirohi, 2013), or provided the local residents with any public services.[14] Nonetheless, by affirming that particular tracts of land are rightly "ours" and not a foreign neighbour's, the BJP builds on its admittedly nationalist ideology and its assertions of a historical "motherland" meant for a specified group of people (Bharatiya Janata Party, 2011). This ideology and accompanying set of assertions is meant to be heard by India's electorate.

The BJP state spokesman's bold declaration and his promise to raise the Indian tricolour in one of the country's exclaves seems to indicate that he is unwilling to give that particular piece of land to Bangladesh, as if he has an autogenous, authentic "connection" with that exclaved spot or that he has a righteous, unalterable understanding of what India "is" in terms of its cartographic shape and therefore always must be.

But in other instances the party seems to be a little more flexible

14. Perhaps with some irony, the BJP's manifesto for recent elections begins with the motto, "To build a prosperous, powerful nation, recall India's past" (Bharatiya Janata Party, 2011).

on what the exact boundaries of India can be, while still maintaining nationalist persona. The BJP, sometimes shouting this down as a "national loss" (*New York Daily News*, 2013), as well as others (Madhav, 2013), have at times argued that India should be compensated in some manner for this net loss of territory, perhaps by Bangladesh ceding or leasing more land around the narrow corridor of West Bengal known as the "chicken's neck" to help cut down on India's transportation costs to its north-east. Yet, discussions of adequate compensation would surely stall the issue further. It would require both sides to identify and agree to new lands they both feel suitable for exchange (Sarkar D., 2013). Bangladesh would also need to ratify an entirely new agreement—at a time when the country is already torn amid contentious domestic politics.

Sengupta (2013) suggests the BJP's dissatisfaction with the LBA is based in electoral calculation. As he sees it, those current enclave residents who would become eligible Indian voters with the ratification of the LBA are more likely to support the Congress Party over the BJP. Therefore, the BJP could be working to preserve a more favourable voters list by stalling efforts to dissolve the South Asian enclaves.

Another openly-stated fear of the LBA's implementation, and thus a potential contributor to its delayed ratification by India, is that it will lead to a large influx of people into the country, straining resources. This has at times been argued by political leaders in West Bengal (Nagchoudhury, 2012; Samanta, 2012). Though not specifically defined in the text of the pending LBA, it is generally understood that the people currently residing in the exclaves of both countries will be given two options: to stay in their present location and become fully-recognised nationals of whichever state they would find themselves following the transfer, or to relocate to the principal territory of either India or Bangladesh (Chaudhury, 2011). Some say that most will choose the option which would allow them to become Indian citizens, as that would provide better socio-economic opportunities than remaining/becoming a Bangladeshi (Sengupta, 2013).

However, Sengupta (2013) does not think that many will choose to physically relocate from India's exclaves in order to remain Indian citizens after implementation. Instead, he believes that most all—in both India's and Bangladesh's exclaves—will choose to remain where they are now. The lives of South Asian enclave residents are intimately connected with the communities currently around them, as he explains, and the cost of purchasing land and starting a whole new life elsewhere in India would be too great to make relocation an attractive option. Sengupta's Bharat Bangladesh Enclave Exchange Coordination Committee reports to have conducted its own census in 2012 of enclave residents, finding that only a small portion of them would choose to move following LBA implementation (Nagchoudhury, 2012). Furthermore, local residents of the Indian exclave Dahala Khagrabari #47 reported in May 2013 that they saw themselves as Bangladeshis, would choose to remain where they are presently, and wished to become Bangladeshi citizens, despite living on sovereign Indian soil and the potential opportunity to become fully Indian citizens.

But fears of a population influx, however unfounded, may not only be connected to logistical or financial concerns for India's ability to adequately meet the needs (with new schools, sanitation utilities, etc.) of thousands of new citizens. Such fears may also be related to ethnic, religious, and linguistic animosities as well. The two members of parliament who stopped the Minister of External Affairs from introducing the land bill in the Rajya Sabha in May are from India's Assam state, a state geographically close to the enclave region and with a history of conflict between ethnic Assamese and Bengali migrants (Baruah, 1986; Baruah, 2009; Kumar A., 2010). It might be that Assamese politicians oppose further settlement of (largely Muslim) Bengalis in "their" territory and thus are opposed to a land transfer agreement they believe will bring many more of them to the area. Certainly, though, Assam would lose control of approximately 1,200 acres of rightly Bangladeshi territory it currently holds in adverse possession with the ratification of the LBA.[15]

15. There are no Bangladeshi exclaves within Assam, nor any Indian exclaves in Bangladesh under the jurisdiction of Assam. All Indian exclaves belong to the state of West Bengal, as noted earlier. However, since 1948, both India and Bangladesh have held small portions of each others' recognised territory under adverse possession. Some of the lands India adversely possesses are governed by Assam.

If Assam loses its adversely-held lands, Sengupta (2013, p. 8) says that it will also lose the thousands of registered voters presently living on those lands. According to him, the LBA's implementation will require these people—now a reliable voting bloc supportive of Assamese political parties—to relocate to Bangladesh. Whatever the root cause of Assamese concern of the LBA, be it continued ethno-nationalist sentiment or the potential loss of a supportive electorate, the state's local politicians have responded to recent efforts to implement the LBA by burning Singh in effigy and threatening the enclave swap would ignite (another) secessionist movement in the state (*The Hindu*, 2013; *The Shillong Times*, 2013).

There has been opposition to the LBA from West Bengal, as well. The state's chief minister, Mamata Banerjee, had in the last couple of years managed to tie the enclaves issue to an unrelated cross-border dispute with neighbouring Bangladesh concerning the sharing of river water. The mighty Teesta River flows through West Bengal before it bisects Bangladesh. With the growing strain on water resources across South Asia, the terms by which bodies of water like the Teesta are used by different states (for drinking water, for irrigation, for hydropower, etc.) has become contentious. It remains unclear whether Banerjee held up a proposed 2011 agreement on river water sharing solely because of her concerns about a possible population influx into her state with the LBA's implementation, conversely whether progress on the LBA was stalled to affect her Teesta negotiations, or even whether both are connected to yet other manoeuvrings, perhaps attempts by West Bengal to extract a larger monetary package from the national government (Ahmed I., 2012; Islam & Akmam, 2010; Samanta, 2012; *The Financial Express*, 2011; Ghosh, 2012). According to Ahmed (2012) there are some who also say that she is holding up the enclaves dissolution to protect non-Bengali business interests in the state, who, as their theory goes, are not keen to have better relations between India and Bangladesh. What is clear is that Banerjee and her party, the All India Trinamool Congress, once opposed implementation of the LBA—for some reason—while they negotiated with Bangladesh and the national government on separate issues, and while being keenly aware of and expressing sympathy for the conditions of enclave residents. These circumstances seem to indicate that the enclaves issue is being used in some manner by Banerjee in connection with other policy matters affecting her state.

Another claim made by opponents to the LBA's implementation is that it would undercut India's position in its separate territorial disputes with Pakistan and China. As their argument suggests, to implement the LBA is to essentially concede that boundaries are flexible, that the sacred Indian Homeland is an imprecise notion or unstable myth, and that political boundaries can simply be changed, even if doing so results in a loss of Indian acreage, to suit broader Indian interests. Concessions like these may make it more difficult for India to argue that it cannot similarly compromise with its other neighbours to settle long-standing territorial disputes. Indeed, an Indian diplomat shared with this author that national legislators were reluctant to support ratification of the LBA at a time when the country was hoping to make strategic gains in its resolution of boundary disputes with China.

Yet there are still other explanations for the LBA's delay occasionally floated. Some for example have blamed corrupt border guards who supposedly have an interest in prolonging the present situation for their own personal gain, while others, including the oldest known resident of the South Asian enclaves, claim the reason for the four-decade delay in India's ratification is because the country has a "boundlessly inefficient" bureaucracy (Institute of Foreign Policy Studies, 2012).

However tedious or disorganised India's bureaucracy may rightly be, it should be remembered that there has been, and continues to be, outright and intentional obstruction of India's efforts to make good on its 1974 accord with Bangladesh. In fact, it is probably not because departmental bureaucrats have just been too slow in filing the correct paperwork, or even that the "enclaves issue" has not been considered enough of a priority for India. Various Indian governments have been trying for nearly half a century to dissolve the enclaves, to mould the country's political geography into a shape more conducive to its own expressed and assumed policy goals. There has long existed, however, an array of competing interests. Those interests seem mostly to stay hidden behind a veil of inaction, unrelated demand, denial, or counter-claim. But every so often, glimpses of those interests can be stolen, as they could that chaotic day in May by the well of the Rajya Sabha.

Stated goals to dissolve the South Asian enclaves may be hamstrung by politicians who leverage their authority to stall ratification of the LBA in order to advance other interests. Similar circumstances exist in Central Asia, but there the nationalist sentiments of the broader public seem to be playing an equally obstructive role.

In fact, it was the leaders of Uzbekistan and Kyrgyzstan who took the initiative to solve their shared enclaves issue once before, but those efforts were stymied by public opposition. In early 2001, Uzbek Prime Minister Utkir Sultanov and Kyrgyz Prime Minister Kurmanbek Bakiev signed a joint memorandum in secret agreeing to proceed with a transfer of territory. According to the agreement, the Kyrgyz Republic was to cede a thin stretch of land to Uzbekistan to connect its Sokh exclave with the country's principal territory. Uzbekistan would cede to the Kyrgyz Republic a corridor to connect Barak to the Kyrgyz homeland in return. The Kyrgyz public and their parliament only found out about the memorandum when it was leaked to the press a few months after the premiers' signing. When they did hear about it, they were outraged, and for several reasons. First, the proposed cession of Kyrgyz lands north of Sokh to the Uzbeks would have cut off a major transportation route to the country's Batken region. The total acreage of land the prime ministers hoped to swap was also unequal, with the Kyrgyz receiving an amount of territory to connect Barak smaller in area than the Uzbek corridor to Sokh. There was of course plenty of anger over the secretive nature of the processes, as well as over leaders acting without consultation with the legislative bodies who actually had the authority to ratify the agreement. But the Kyrgyz public was also upset that any agreement was being forged with a foreign neighbour who had been so hostile to their country in the months and years prior. The agreement to physically connect the territories (and thus end their enclaved status) promptly died (Dadabaev, 2012; International Crisis Group, 2002; Passon & Temirkulov, 2004; Utyaganova, 2001). The International Crisis Group (2002, p. 15) summarised the resulting, longer-term effects of the 2001 affair by noting:

> "Public anger over the clandestine border talks [between Sultanov and Bakiev] also constrained President Akaev's ability to make future territorial concessions."

The poorly orchestrated attempt at solving two troublesome enclave cases emboldened domestic nationalist opposition in the Kyrgyz Republic and twisted Uzbek-Kyrgyz relations, no doubt making it difficult for the two countries to hold constructive discussions on a more rational political geography that would surely be in both their interests.

With a land corridor off the table, the Kyrgyz government was then considered to have only one other option for improving the living conditions of those in its Barak exclave: move them (Radio Free Europe/ Radio Liberty, 2003). It was mentioned earlier that the Kyrgyz government made land available in the mainland for a portion of Barak's residents, but that it may have intended to keep some in the exclave so as to maintain a claim to the isolated territory. The possibility of dissolving the enclaves shared between Uzbekistan and Kyrgyzstan, in a manner similar to plans in South Asia, does not appear to have ever been seriously explored by either government.

One reason the two countries seem intent on keeping their enclaves is their strategic resource value to their home state. Recall that the enclaves were initially created because Soviet republics needed various resources located inside another republic's jurisdiction, and so they leased pockets of land from a neighbour to provide them access to those resources. The same principles apply today, but in the rigid confines of an internationalised system. While the enclaves of South Asia provide little meaningful access to natural resources for either India or Bangladesh, at least some of the enclaves of Central Asia are still useful to their respective governments for water, grazing, and even energy. Myrzabekova and Sikorskaya (2013) explain that Uzbekistan continues to use Sokh to access natural gas deposits in the Ferghana Valley region. With water a scarce and highly-valued commodity in Central Asia, access to rivers is also critically important—and a reason to hold on tightly to the access you already have (Maynes, 2003; Utyaganova, 2001). Sokh's resource value contributes to its overall "high strategic value" for Uzbekistan, which, in the minds of the country's policymakers, trumps the value of promoting regional cooperation (Passon & Temirkulov, 2004, p. 62).

Bureaucratic inefficiency does not appear to be a major contributor to India's delays in ratifying the 1974 LBA, though Myrzabekova and Sikorskaya (2013) convincingly identify some procedural challenges which could be stymieing progress to lay down more agreeable boundaries in Central Asia. As they explain, Uzbekistan's "rigidly hierarchical" system of governance firmly controlled by the autocratic President Islam Kharimov does not allow the country's diplomats much flexibility in negotiations over border concerns with Bishkek. Instead, the Uzbek negotiators must always seek the approval of higher up officials before reaching even a minor agreement, delaying the process.

Earlier it was posited that fears of creating a disadvantageous precedent in separate boundary disputes work to preserve the enclaves in South Asia. In settling a boundary agreement with China, the government of Kyrgyzstan ended its claim to nearly a quarter million acres of territory along its eastern frontier. Sukhov (2002) argues that acquiescence to the Chinese position in this settlement can be leveraged by Uzbekistan in its ongoing negotiations over boundaries and enclave ownership with Kyrgyzstan. While deft Kyrgyz may be able to effectively separate the Chinese and Uzbek border circumstances, their forgoing of large tracts of territory does undermine the contention that boundaries once claimed are forever authoritative and not amendable.

Conclusion

This paper had two main goals, the first to demonstrate, with a comparison of the political geography of two regions, that the existence of true enclaves in South and Central Asia undermines the stated policy goals and assumed broader interests of the states who both lay claim to and encase them. The second goal was to enumerate possible explanations for these disconnected territories' continued existence, despite their infestive effects on public health and education, economic development, national and regional security, gender equality, communal stability, and individuals' basic dignity. In so doing, this paper aimed to clarify relevant terminology and the historical origins of particular case studies.

The enclaves of South and Central Asia have many similar characteristics and several analogous consequences for their respective residents and states. All the enclaves considered in this paper exercise a largely agrarian economy and lack the same standards of public infrastructure and services available in their states' mainlands. Such conditions result not just from these territories' physical isolation, but more specifically from the recent internationalisation of their long-existent boundaries, as well as from the imposition of modern, inflexible notions of territorial sovereignty in two regions with complex political geography. Poor—indeed, inhumane—living standards in South and Central Asia's enclaves prevents their nominally sovereign national governments from fully achieving their explicit policy goals and living up to its legitimising commitments on a number of fronts.

However, the remaining differences between the enclaves of South Asia and Central Asia are the result of dissimilar administration and manifestation in physical space. All but one of the enclaves of South Asia, which are far more numerous than those in Central Asia, are unfenced, despite the precise location of their boundaries being fully known and agreed to. Their porous, mostly unguarded, borders allow residents to move in and out at least physically unobstructed in order to engage in the commerce and society of the surrounding community. However, these enclave residents lack official identification documents, a circumstance which leaves them unable to access even the most basic services in any location.

The exact number of true enclaves in Central Asia is disputed, as are the exact location of even the known-enclaves' boundaries. It is this uncertainty, coupled with the efforts of states driven by cross-border suspicion and rivalry to fence, guard, block, and even mine their disputed enclave edges that has seeded such hardship in this region. Yet the residents of Central Asia's enclaves are afforded official identification, and to an occasional and albeit minor degree, are provided with at least some minimal public services. Some living in Barak have even been helped by their national government to relocate.

It seems in South Asia that the short-sighted goals of a few state and national politicians are working to preserve the region's enclaves, despite broad national commitments over decades to see to their dissolution. Conversely, a pair of leaders in Central Asia had once narrowly and secretly attempted to resolve their own countries' enclaves issue, but were swamped by popular opposition, charged conceptions of nationalism, and the assertion that the enclaves play a vital strategic role for their states.

Yet this paper has shown how, on balance, the maintenance of the enclaves are not in the interests of states in either South or Central Asia, and therefore should be merged with the territory of their surrounding state. Doing so would not be entirely unprecedented, either. In 1995, the governments of Lithuania and Belarus, having recognised the resulting administrative difficulties, signed a revised border agreement that saw the dissolution of a Lithuanian exclave inside of Belarus in exchange for an equal-sized piece of Belorussian territory elsewhere (Krogh, 2010; *The Lithuanian Tribune*, 2012). It was argued earlier that negotiations over transferring enclave territories in South Asia, or elsewhere for that matter, should not be delayed because of a relatively minor imbalance in the prospective net gain of acreage; it is in India's interests to ratify the 1974 LBA in its present form without compensation for the 10,000 acres of territory it would then lose sovereignty over. Nonetheless, the Lithuania-Belarus example shows that it is possible for states to relax notions of territorial sovereignty and actively choose to draw more rational, administratively feasible boundaries in order to achieve larger and more important policy goals.

Further research is necessary to understand how the forces obstructing such geographic rationality in South and Central Asia can be overcome. Work must also be done to understand the logistical steps required to meet the needs of enclave residents following any exchange of territory. This will include an analysis of the costs and time necessary to build basic infrastructure in the then formerly-enclaved territories, as well as the issuance of identification documents. Such preparations can begin now, however, and should not wait for the regions' respective governments to choose to redraw the boundaries they inherited.

Maps Annex

The enclaves of the Central Asia are shared between Kyrgyzstan, Tajikistan, and Uzbekistan. Note that in this map the most common transliterations are used for the enclaves' names and that the existence of Tayan as an exclave of Uzbekistan is not fully recognised among scholars or government representatives.

Map 1: Melilla is a pene-exclave of Spain. It is accessible to the Spanish "mainland" directly by crossing the Mediterranean Sea without having to cross the shared land boundary with Morocco.

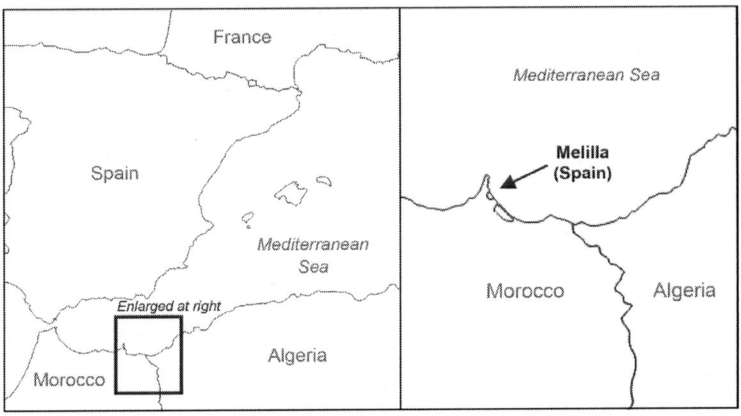

Map 2: Lesotho is an enclaved state entirely surrounded by the enclaving state of South Africa.

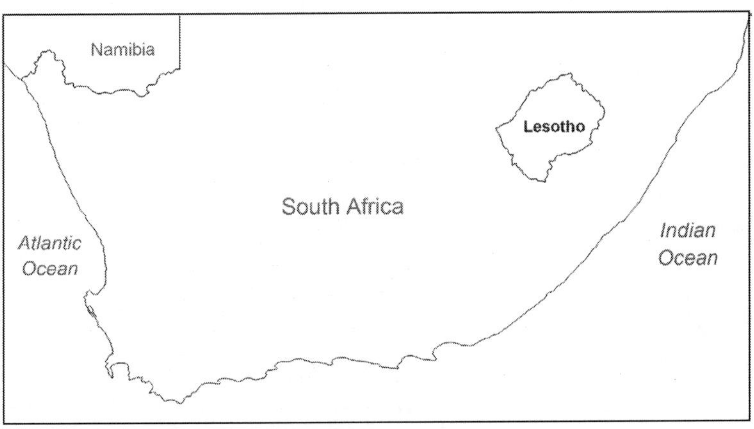

Map 3: The Nakhchivan Autonomous Republic consists of the larger territory diagrammed above, as well as the smaller village of Tigranashen. The larger portion is an exclave of the principal territory of Azerbaijan, but is not an enclave as it shares boundaries with Armenia, Iran, and Turkey. Tigranashen is at once a true enclave, an exclave of Azerbaijan, and an exclave of Azerbaijan's Nakhchivan Autonomous Republic. Tigranashen is said to be enclaved by Armenia.

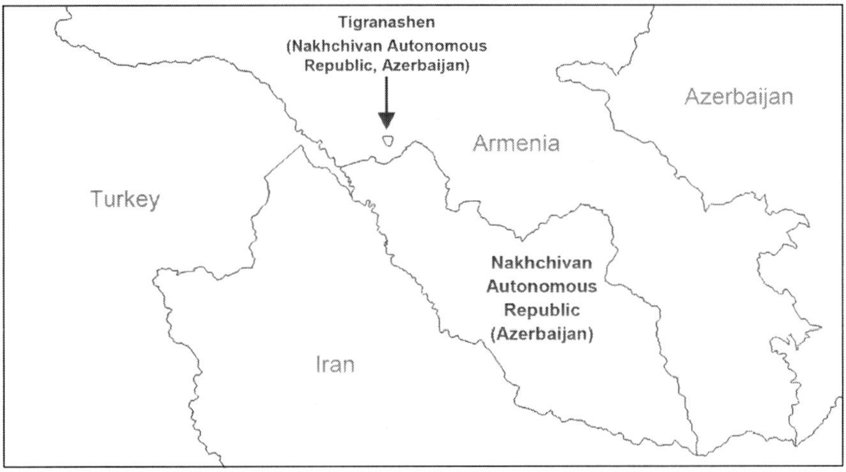

Map 4: San Marino and the Vatican City are both enclaved states, as they are entirely surrounded by the sovereign territory of Italy. They are not, however, true enclaves.

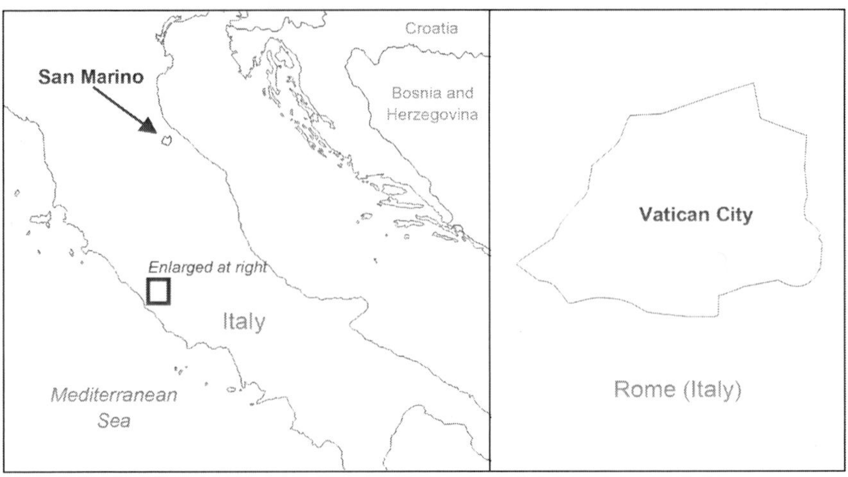

Map 5: Point Roberts, a *pene-exclave* of the USA, is directly accessible to the rest of its country by sea. Accessing the territory by land requires passing through Canada. It is not an *enclave*.

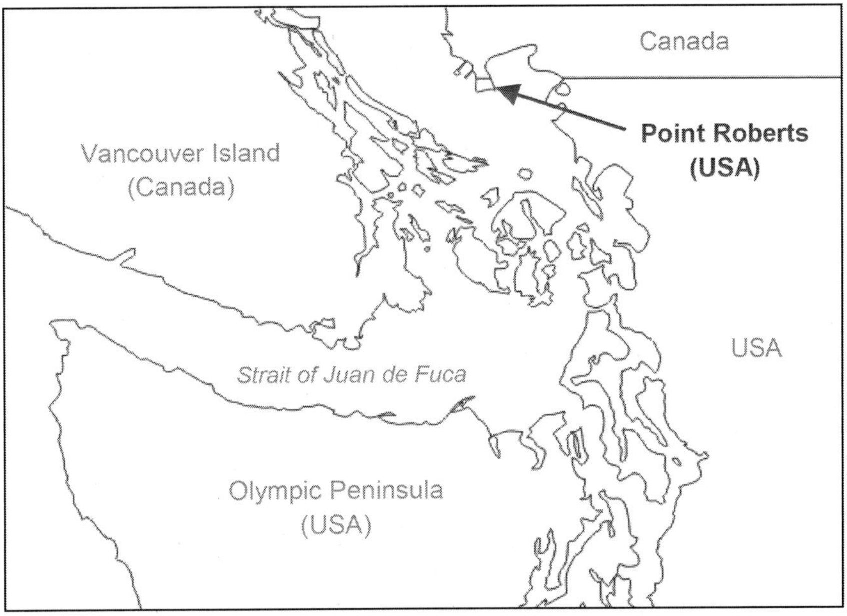

Map 6: Kaliningrad Oblast, a *pene-exclave* of Russia, is directly accessible to its "homeland" via the Baltic Sea, or by land by passing through at least two other countries. It is not an *enclave*.

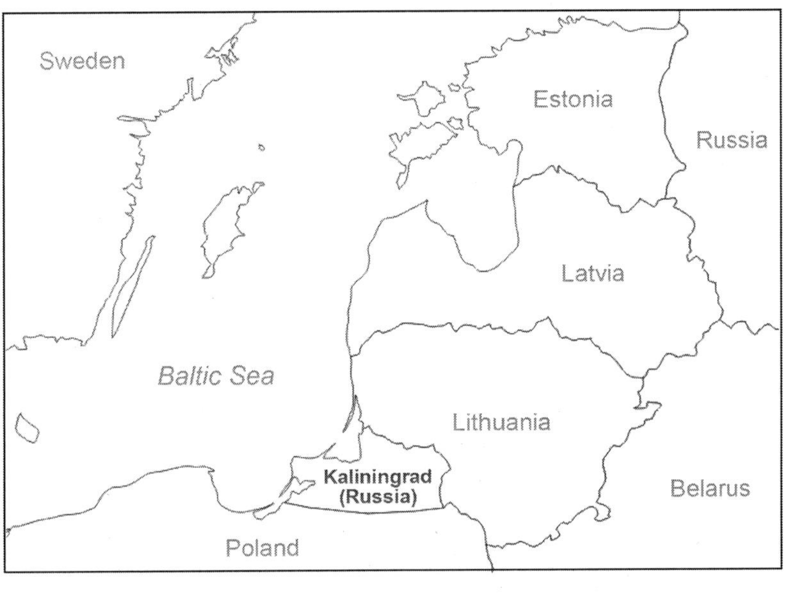

Map 7: The 198 true enclaves of South Asia along the India-Bangladesh border.

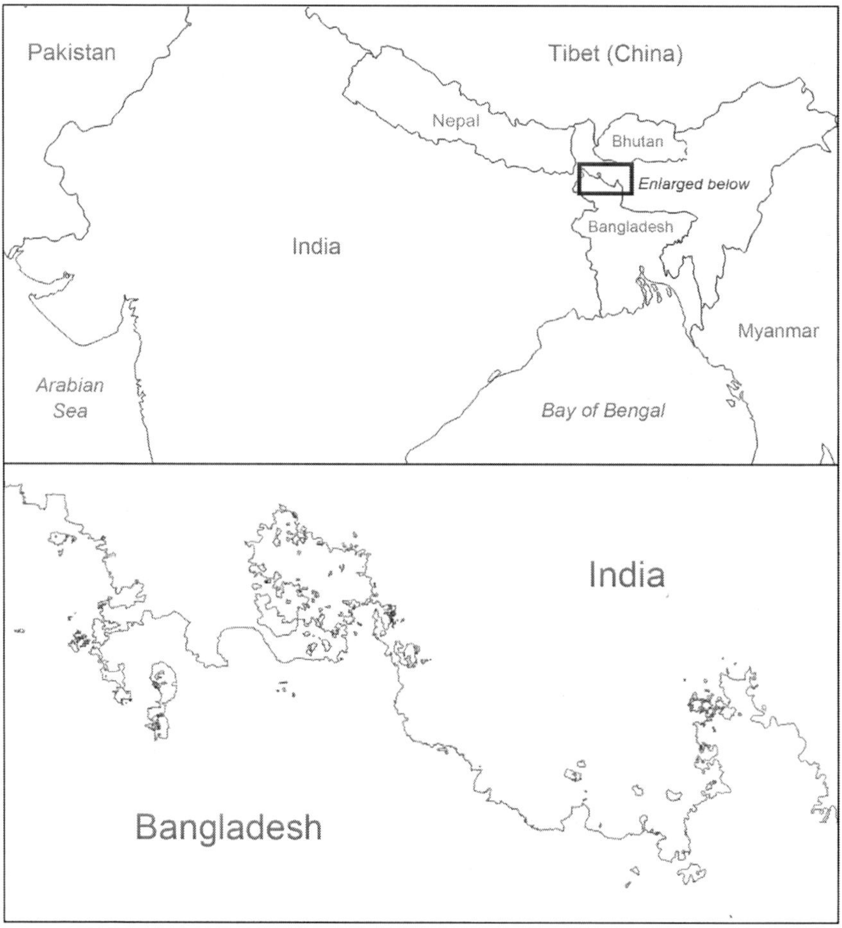

Map 8 (Right): Bangladesh's Dahagram-Angarpota exclave is connected to the Bangladeshi mainland via the Tin Bigha Corridor, a sovereign strip of Indian territory.

Map 9: The enclaves of the Central Asia are shared between Kyrgyzstan, Tajikistan, and Uzbekistan. Note that in this map the most common transliterations are used for the enclaves' names and that the existence of Tayan as an exclave of Uzbekistan is not fully recognised among scholars or government representatives.

Bibliography

Adanov, R. 2013, June 18. First Secretary, Embassy of the Kyrgyz Republic in Washington, DC. Personal email.

Ahmed, I. 2012. "Teesta, Tipaimukh and River Linking: Danger to Bangladesh-India Relations." *Economic and Political Weekly*, XLVII: 16, 51-53.

Ahmed, R. 2009. "Interface of Political Opportunism and Islamic Extremism in Bangladesh: Rhetorical Identification in Government Response." *Communication Studies*, 60:1, 82-96.

Akhmadov, E. 2013, January 23. "Tensions continue in Sokh enclave, Uzbekistan." Retrieved June 24, 2013, from Central Asia-Caucasus Institute: http://old.cacianalyst.org/?q=node/5917.

AKIpress News Agency. 2013, January 23. "Uzbekistan blocks Kyrgyz enclave Barak." Retrieved June 22, 2013, from The Free Library: http://www.thefreelibrary.com/Uzbekistan+blocks+Kyrgyz+enclave+Barak.-a0315993059.

Al Jazeera News. 2013, May 7. "Police ban rallies in Dhaka after violence." Retrieved June 16, 2013, from *Al Jazeera English*: www.aljazeera.com/news/asia/2013/05/2013576457765572.html.

Asia Society. 2011. "Indian Society and Ways of Living: Organization of Social Life in India." Retrieved June 28, 2013, from Asia Society: http://asiasociety.org/countries/traditions/indian-society-and-ways-living.

Asiatic Society of Bangladesh. 2006. "About the Asiatic Society of Bangladesh." Retrieved June 19, 2013, from Asiatic Society of Bangladesh: http://www.asiaticsociety.org.bd/index.htm.

———. 2006. "Enclave." Retrieved June 20, 2013, from Banglapedia: http://www.banglapedia.org/HT/E_0054.HTM.

———. 2006. Publications of the Asiatic Society of Bangladesh. Retrieved June 19, 2013, from Asiatic Society of Bangladesh: http://www.asiaticsociety.org.bd/publication.htm.

Aspen Institute India. (n.d.). "India-Bangladesh Relations: Towards Increased Partnership." Retrieved June 28, 2013, from Aspen India: http://www.aspenindia.org/pdf/India_Bangladesh_Report.pdf.

Aydarov, J. 2009, April 10. "Kyrgyz, Tajiks Place High Value on Scrap of Land." Retrieved June 22, 2013, from Institute for War and Peace Reporting: http://iwpr.net/report-news/kyrgyz-tajiks-place-high-value-scrap-land.

Baghirov, A. M. 2012. "The Leading Role of Industry in the Nakhchivan Autonomous Republic." *International Journal of Economics and Finance*, 4:11, 210-16.

Barbhuiya, S. 2009. "India-Bangladesh Relations: Issues and Challenges." Himalayan and Central Asian Studies, 13:4, 35-62.

Bartholomew, J. G. 1893. *Constable's Hand Atlas of India*. India: A. Constable Westminster.

Baruah, S. 1986. "Immigration, Ethnic Conflict, and Political Turmoil—Assam, 1979-1985." Asian Survey, 26:11, 1184-1206.

Baruah, S. 2009. "Separatist Militants and Contentious Politics in Assam, India: The Limits of Counterinsurgency." *Asian Survey*, 49:6, 951-74.

BBC News. 2013, March 21. In pictures: Lives in limbo on India-Bangladesh border. Retrieved June 24, 2013, from BBC News: http://www.bbc.co.uk/news/world-asia-india-21144694.

Berg, N. 2012, February 17. "The Odd Existence of Point Roberts, Washington." Retrieved July 1, 2013, from *The Atlantic Cities*: http://www.theatlanticcities.com/neighborhoods/2012/02/strange-existence-point-roberts-washington/1265/.

Bharatiya Janata Party. 2011. "BJP Manifesto: Lok Sabha Elections 2009." Retrieved July 4, 2013, from Bharatiya Janata Party: http://www.bjp.org/index.php?option=com_content&view=article&id=137:manifesto-lok-sabha-election-2009&catid=50:election-manifestos&Itemid=549.

Bharatiya Janata Party. 2011. "Hindutva: The Great Nationalist Ideology." Retrieved July 4, 2013, from Bharatiya Janata Party: http://www.bjp.org/index.php?option=com_content&view=article&id=369:hindutva-the-great-nationalist-ideology&catid=92&Itemid=501.

Bhasin, A. S. 2011. "India's Foreign Relations—2011: Documents." Retrieved June 27, 2013, from Ministry of External Affairs: www.mea.gov.in/Images/pdf/India-foreign-relation-2011.pdf.

Biswas, A. K. 2000, July 3. "A Place without a Place." Retrieved June 28, 2013, from *Outlook India*: http://www.outlookindia.com/article.aspx?209622.

Bose, R. 2011, July 19. "Census in Indian and Bangladesh enclaves ends." Retrieved June 26, 2013, from *The Hindu*: http://www.thehindu.com/news/national/census-in-indian-and-bangladesh-enclaves-ends/article2260223.ece.

Cembalest, R. 1997. "Spain's African Enclave." *New Leader*, 80:13, 9.

Centre for Study of Society and Secularism. 2011. "Status of Women in India: Problems and Concerns." Internship Project (December 2010-January 2011). Mumbai: Centre for Study of Society and Secularism.

Chaki, D. 2011. Brattajaner Brittanta Prasanga Bharat-Bangladesh Chhitmahal [Investigative Essays on Indo-Bangla Enclaves]. Kolkata: Sotan.

Chakrabarty, R. 2013, May 8. "AGP MPs bar Khurshid from introducing Bill to ratify boundary pact with Bangladesh." Retrieved. June 16, 2013, from *The Times of India*: http://articles.timesofindia.indiatimes.com/2013-05-08/india/39115169_1_congress-mps-bjp-mps-law-minister-ashwani-kumar.

Chaudhury, D. R. 2011, September 7. "India, Bangladesh settle boundary dispute." Retrieved June 16, 2013, from *India Today*: http://indiatoday.intoday.in/story/india-bangladesh-settle-boundary-dispute/1/150380.html.

Cobbe, J. H. 1988. "Economic Aspects of Lesotho's Relations with South Africa." *The Journal of Modern African Studies*, 26:1, 71-89.

Cohen, A. 2004, August 5. "Terror in Tashkent." Retrieved June 30, 2013, from The Heritage Foundation: http://www.heritage.org/research/commentary/2004/08/terror-in-tashkent.

Cons, J. 2012. "Histories of Belonging(s): Narrating Territory, Possession, and Dispossession at the India-Bangladesh Border." *Modern Asian Studies*, 46:3, 527-58.

Dadabaev, T. 2012. "Securing Central Asian Frontiers: Institutionalisation of Borders and Inter-State Relations." *Strategic Analysis*, 36:4, 554-68.

Das Kundu, N. 2003. "Kaliningrad: Russian Enclave in the European Union." *Strategic Analysis*, 27:4, 626-42.

Datta, R. 2011, April 17. "Voters in Bangladeshi enclaves seek to establish their identity." Retrieved June 24, 2013, from Live Mint & the Wall Street Journal: http://www.livemint.com/Politics/X01wRY6bq1AdqugVF0FQDJ/Voters-in-Bangladeshi-enclaves-seek-to-establish-their-iden.html.

Deccan Herald. 2011, August 30. "Historic India-Bangladesh enclaves' swap next week." Retrieved June 22, 2013, from *Deccan Herald*: http://www.deccanherald.com/content/187474/historic-india-bangladesh-enclaves-swap.html.

———. 2013, June 12. "India assures Bangladesh over Teesta water sharing treaty." Retrieved June 27, 2013, from *Deccan Herald*: http://www.deccanherald.com/content/338282/india-assures-bangladesh-over-teesta.html.

Department of Border Management. 2012, July 11. "Introduction." Retrieved June 25, 2013, from Ministry of Home Affairs (Department of Border Management): http://mha.nic.in/docs/BM_Intro(E)050110.doc.

Department of Commerce. 2012. "Strategic Plan." Retrieved June 25, 2013, from Department of Commerce: http://commerce.nic.in/ann/StrategicPlan.pdf.

Department of Health and Family Welfare. 2013. RFD (Results Framework Document) For Department of Health and Family Welfare (2013-14). Retrieved June 25, 2013, from Department of Health and Family Welfare, Government of India: http://mohfw.nic.in/showfile.php?lid=1527.

Department of Industrial Policy and Promotion. 2008. "Mission." Retrieved June 25, 2013, from Department of Industrial Policy and Promotion, Ministry of Commerce and Industry: http://dipp.nic.in/English/AboutUs/Mission.aspx.

Department of Information Technologies and Electronics. 2012. "West Bengal Policy on Information & Communication Technology, 2012." Retrieved June 27, 2013, from Department of Information Technologies and Electronics, Government of West Bengal: http://www.itwb.org/presentations%20&%20all%20%20PDF/West%20Bengal%20Policy%202012.pdf.

Department of Power and Non-Conventional Energy Sources. (n.d.). "Introduction." Retrieved June 27, 2013, from Department of Power and Non-Conventional Energy Sources, Government of West Bengal: http://www.wbpower.nic.in/.

Department of School Education and Literacy. 2013, May 30. "Overview." Retrieved June 25, 2013, from Department of School Education and Literacy, Ministry of Human Resource Development: http://mhrd.gov.in/elementaryeducation1.

———. 2012, November 8. "Right to Education." Retrieved June 25, 2013, from Department of School Education and Literacy, Ministry of Human Resource Development: http://mhrd.gov.in/rte.

Dessì, A. 2012. "Shifting Sands: Security and Development for Egypt's Sinai." Washington: The German Marshall Fund of the United States and Istituto Affari Internazionali.

Division of Community and Regional Affairs. 2012. Hyder. Retrieved July 1, 2013, from Communities, Division of Community and Regional Affairs, State of Alaska: http://

commerce.alaska.gov/cra/DCRAExternal/community/Details/2dce25e6-732b-4475-82fd-1a31f090239f.

Division of Community and Regional Affairs. 2012. Klukwan. Retrieved July 6, 2013, from Division of Community and Regional Affairs, State of Alaska: http://commerce.salaska.gov/cra/DCRAExternal/Community/Details/0baf70be-c0aa-4053-8d87-e9bcabae2bf8.

Dodds, K. 2010. "Kyrgyzstan." *Geographical*, 82:5, 14.

Dudka, I. 2013, February 19. "Kyrgyzstan negotiates with Uzbekistan over simplified border crossing for Barak residents." Retrieved June 29, 2013, from 24.kg: http://eng.24.kg/business/2013/02/19/26034.html.

Dutta, N. 2011, September 10. "Demystifying the Claims and Counter-Claims of the Indo Bangladesh Border Settlement in Assam." Retrieved June 16, 2013, from Chanakya's Neeti: http://chanakyasneeti.wordpress.com/2011/09/10/demystifying-the-claims-and-counter-claims-of-the-indo-bangladesh-border-settlement-in-assam/.

Edward, O. 2013, February. "The United States of Nowhere." Retrieved June 20, 2013, from Geographical: http://www.geographical.co.uk/Magazine/Cooch_Behar_enclaves_-_Feb_13.html.

Efendiev, A. 1999. "Azerbaijan: Enormous potential and challenging economic opportunities." *European Business Journal*, 11:4, 176.

Epprecht, M. 1995. "Democratizing the southern African past." *Canadian Journal of History*, 30:2, 323-27.

Espach, R. and D. Haering. 2012. *Border Insecurity in Central America's Northern Triangle*. Washington: Migration Policy Institute.

Farran, C. D. 1955. "International Enclaves and Question of State Servitudes." *The International and Comparative Law Quarterly*, 4:2, 294-307.

Fitzpatrick, C. A. 2010, June 25. "Uzbekistan Weekly Roundup." Retrieved June 24, 2013, from Eurasianet.org: http://www.eurasianet.org/node/61406.

Gelbman, A. and D. J. Timothy. 2011. "Border complexity, tourism, and international exclaves: A case study." *Annals of Tourism Research*, vol. 38, no. 1, 110-31.

Ghosh, R. 2012, August 3. "Diptiman Sengupta: Residents of Indian and Bangladeshi enclaves are stateless." Retrieved July 4, 2013, from *The Times of India*: http://articles.timesofindia.indiatimes.com/2012-08-03/interviews/33002254_1_enclaves-diptiman-sengupta-land-boundary-agreement.

———. 2013, May 21. "India's nowhere people." Retrieved June 16, 2013, from *The Times of India*: http://blogs.timesofindia.indiatimes.com/talkingturkey/entry/india-s-nowhere-people#comments.

Government of Batken Oblast. 2010. Общая информация о Баткенской области [General Information About the Batken Region]. Retrieved June 30, 2013, from Government of Batken Oblast: http://batken.e-region.kg/Articles/ViewArticle.aspx?id=230.

Government of India Department of Administrative Reforms & Public Grievances. 2013,

February 14. "Union Cabinet approves amendment bill on India-Bangladesh Land Boundary Agreement, 1974." Retrieved June 16, 2013, from Governance Knowledge Centre: http://indiagovernance.gov.in/news.php?id=1995.

Government of West Bengal. 2011, September 17. "State Water Policy." Kolkata, West Bengal, India: Government of West Bengal.

Gupta, A. 2010. "Tasks before Indian Foreign Policy." *Strategic Analysis*, 35:1, 1-5.

Gupta, S. 2011, October 10. "India and Bangladesh: Calculus of territorial dispute settlement." Retrieved June 27, 2013, from *East Asia Forum*: http://www.eastasiaforum.org/2011/10/10/india-and-bangladesh-calculus-of-territorial-dispute-settlement/

Habib, H. 2003, October 26. "Insurgents receiving support in Bangladesh: Indian envoy." Retrieved June 27, 2013, from *The Hindu*: http://www.hindu.com/2003/10/26/stories/2003102604511000.htm

Harrington, J. 2010. *Sir John Malcolm and the Creation of British India*. New York: Palgrave Macmillan.

Hartley, A. C. 1940. Final Report of the Rangpur Survey and Settlement Operations 1931-1938. Calcutta: Bengal Government Press, Alipore.

High Commision of India. 1974, May 16. Agreement between the Government of the Republic of India and Government of the People's Republic of Bangladesh concerning the demarcation of the land boundary between India and Bangladesh and related matters, May 16, 1974. Retrieved January 2, 2013, from High Commision of India: Dhaka, Bangladesh: www.hcidhaka.org/agreement_india_bd.php.

———. 1974, May 16. High Commision of India: Dhaka, Bangladesh. Retrieved January 2, 2013, from Agreement between the Government of the Republic of India and Government of the People's Republic of Bangladesh concerning the demarcation of the land boundary between India and Bangladesh and related matters, May 16, 1974: www.hcidhaka.org/agreement_india_bd.php.

Hirsch, F. 2000. "Toward an Empire of Nations: Border-Making and the Formation of Soviet National Identities." *Russian Review*, 59:2, 201-26.

Hoggarth, J. 2012. Azerbaijan. *New Internationalist*, 454, 18.

Ibbotson, S., and M. Lovell-Hoare. 2010. "Bishkek and the Great Game." *Russian Life*, 53:5, 26-33.

Institute of Foreign Policy Studies. 2012, July 9. "Chitmahal Interaction." Kolkata, West Bengal, India.

International Crisis Group. 2002. Central Asia: Border Disputes and Conflict Potential, ICG Asia Report No. 33. Osh/Brussels: International Crisis Group.

International Monetary Fund. 2012, May. "Kyrgyz Republic: Medium-Term Development Program—Poverty Reduction Strategy Paper." Retrieved July 1, 2013, from International Monetary Fund, Publications: www.imf.org/external/pubs/ft/scr/2012/cr12112.pdf.

———. 2007, June. "Kyrgyz Republic: Poverty Reduction Strategy Paper—Country Development Strategy (2007-2010)." Retrieved June 16, 2013, from International

Monetary Fund, Publications: http://www.imf.org/external/pubs/ft/scr/2007/cr07193.pdf.

IRIN News Service. 2004, November 1. "Kyrgyzstan-Uzbekistan: Demining around Uzbek enclaves brings hope to impoverished villagers." Retrieved June 30, 2013, from IRIN News Service: http://www.irinnews.org/indepthmain.aspx?InDepthId=19&ReportId=62816.

———. 2005. "Tough life in Barak enclave." Retrieved June 18, 2013, from IRIN News Service: http://www.irinnews.org/fr/report/29113/kyrgyzstan-tough-life-in-barak-enclave.

———. 2001, June 5. "Uzbekistan: IRIN Focus on ethnic enclaves in Ferghana Valley." Retrieved June 23, 2013, from IRIN News Service: http://www.irinnews.org/report/14922/uzbekistan-irin-focus-on-ethnic-enclaves-in-ferghana-valley.

Islam, F. and W. Akmam. 2010. "Ethical Aspects of Sharing International River Water: The Case of Teesta River." *Bangladesh Journal of Bioethics*, 1:6.

Jacobs, S. M. 2013, June 20. Cultural Affairs Officer, Embassy of the United States in Dushanbe. Personal email.

———. 2013, June 19. Cultural Affairs Officer, Embassy of the United States in Dushanbe. Personal email.

Jafarova, A. 2013, January 23. "Uzbekistan, Kyrgyzstan avoid large-scale conflict." Retrieved June 16, 2013, from Azernews: http://www.azernews.az/analysis/48703.html.

Jamestown Foundation. 2013, May 28. "Nine Potential 'Karabakhs' in Central Asia Heating Up." Retrieved June 16, 2013, from *Refworld*, UNHCR: http://www.refworld.org/docid/51a736234.html.

Jamoat Resource Centre of Vorukh. 2011, July. "Potential for Peace and Threats of Conflict: Development Analysis of Cross-Border Communities in Isfara District of the Republic of Tajikistan (Vorukh, Chorukhuh, Surkh, Shurab) and Batken District of the Kyrgyz Republic (Ak-Sai, Ak-Tatyr, Samarkandek)." Retrieved June 22, 2013, from United Nations Development Programme in Tajikistan: www.undp.tj/files/Report%20in%20English(2).pdf.

Jones, R. 2009. "Sovereignty and statelessness in the border enclaves of India and Bangladesh." *Political Geography*, 28, 373-81.

Kaiser, R. and L. Raimondo. 2002, July 15. "The Volatile Fergana Valley." Retrieved June 22, 2013, from *Washington Post* via West Chester University: http://courses.wcupa.edu/rbove/eco343/024Compecon/Soviet/Asia/020715Fergana.txt

Karim, R. 2011, February 20. "Dhaka, Delhi move to swap enclaves." Retrieved June 20, 2013, from *The Daily Star*: http://archive.thedailystar.net/newDesign/news-details.php?nid=174764.

Khamidov, A. 2009, August 12. "Fergana Valley: Stringent Border Measures Fuelling Tension in Enclaves." Retrieved June 30, 2013, from Eurasianet.org: http://www.eurasianet.org/departments/insightb/articles/eav081309.shtml.

———. 2008, June 1. "Ferghana Valley: Harsh Winter's Legacy Stokes Ethnic Tension." Retrieved June 24, 2013, from Eurasianet.org: http://www.eurasianet.org/

departments/insight/articles/eav060208.shtml.

———. 2011, April 20. "Kyrgyzstan-Tajikistan: Clashes on Volatile Border Growing Vicious." Retrieved June 24, 2013, from Eurasianet.org: http://www.eurasianet.org/node/63336.

Kimsanov, M. 2003, June 5. "Residents of Kyrgyz Enclave in Uzbekistan Feel Like Castaways." Retrieved January 5, 2013, from Eurasianet: http://www.eurasianet.org/departments/insight/articles/eav060603.shtml.

Kishor, S. and K. Gupta. 2009, August. "National Family Health Survey (NFHS-3), India, 2005-06: Gender Equity and Women's Empowerment in India." Retrieved June 28, 2013, from Ministry of Health and Family Welfare, Government of India: http://www.measuredhs.com/pubs/pdf/OD57/OD57.pdf.

Kokaisl, P. and P. Kokaislová. 2009. "The Kyrgyz—Children of Manas." Prague: Nostalgie Praha.

Kothari, J. 2006. "The Right to Water: A Constitutional Perspective." Delhi: International Environmental Law Research Centre, "Water, Law and the Commons" Workshop.

Krogh, J. 2010, April 1. "Former Lithuanian exclave of Pagiriai." Retrieved July 7, 2013, from http://geosite.jankrogh.com/enklaver/pagiriai/pagiriai.htm.

Kumar, A. 2010. "Illegal Bangladeshi Migration to India: Impact on Internal Security." *Strategic Analysis*, 35:1, 106-19.

———. 2009. "Rethinking State Politics in India: Regions within Regions." *Economic and Political Weekly*, 44:19, 14-19.

———. 2010. "Sheikh Hasina's Visit to India and the Future of Indo-Bangladesh Relations." Asian Affairs, 41:3, 422-35.

Lewis, D. 2012, September. "India Economic Growth: Once a Shining Economy, India is in Danger of Running Out of Gas." Retrieved June 25, 2013, from PolicyMic: http://www.policymic.com/articles/16089/india-economic-growth-once-a-shining-economy-india-is-in-danger-of-running-out-of-gas.

Lok Sabha Thirteenth Session. 2013. Fifteenth Series, Vol. XXXI, Thirteenth Session, 2013/1934 (Saka), No. 2, Friday, February 22, 2013/Phalguna 03, 1934 (Saka). Lok Sabha Debates Proceedings (pp. 1-118). Delhi: Lok Sabha.

Madhav, R. 2013, April 20. "Ram Madhav writes: Govt. Must Renegotiate Pending Issues in Indira-Mujib Accord before ratifying it." Retrieved July 4, 2013, from Vishwa Samvada Kendra, Karnataka: http://samvada.org/2013/news/ram-madhav-writes-govt-must-renegotiate-pending-issues-in-indira-mujib-accord-before-ratifying-it/.

Maynes, C. W. 2003. "America Discovers Central Asia." *Foreign Affairs*, 82:2, 120-32.

McAllister, B. 1996, May 14. "Canadians Find Shelter in US Border Enclave." *The Washington Post*, p. A3.

Megoran, N. 2012. "Rethinking the Study of International Boundaries: A Biography of the Kyrgyzstan-Uzbekistan Boundary." *Annals of the Association of American Geographers*, 102:2, 464-81.

Metcalf, B. and T. Metcalf. 2012. *A Concise History of Modern India*. Cambridge: Cambridge University Press.

Ministry of Foreign Affairs of the Kyrgyz Republic. 2013. Minister of Foreign Affairs of the

Kyrgyz Republic Erlan Abdyldaev met with Minister of Foreign Affairs of the Republic of Tajikistan Hamrohon Zarifi. Retrieved June 16, 2013, from Ministry of Foreign Affairs of the Kyrgyz Republic: http://www.mfa.kg/mews-of-mfa-kr/ministr-inostrannih-del-kr-a.abdildaev-vstretilsya-s-glavoi-mid-rt-h.zarifi_en.html.

Ministry of Home Affairs. 2012, July 11. "Border Area Development Programme." Retrieved June 25, 2013, from Ministry of Home Affairs (Department of Border Management): http://mha.nic.in/pdfs/BADP.pdf.

———. 2012, July 11. IX. "Border Area Development Programme." Retrieved June 25, 2013, from Ministry of Home Affairs (Department of Border Management): mha.nic.in/pdfs/BM_BADP(E).pdf.

Ministry of Human Resource Development. 2012, February 3. About MHRD: Overview. Retrieved June 25, 2013, from Ministry of Human Resource Development, Government of India: http://mhrd.gov.in/node/16.

Ministry of Women and Child Development. (n.d.). "National Policy for the Empowerment of Women (2001)." Retrieved June 28, 2013, from Ministry of Women and Child Development, Government of India: http://wcd.nic.in/empwomen.htm.

Myrzabekova, A. and I. Sikorskaya. 2013, February 15. "Enclave Issues Challenge Uzbek, Kyrgyz Leaders." Retrieved June 16, 2013, from Institute for War & Peace Reporting: http://iwpr.net/report-news/enclave-issues-challenge-uzbek-kyrgyz-leaders.

Nagchoudhury, S. 2012, June 19. "If enclaves are exchanged, only a handful will want to move." Retrieved December 21, 2012, from *The Indian Express*: http://www.indianexpress.com/news/if-enclaves-are-exchanged-only-a-handful-will-want-to-move/963636.

Narcotics Control Bureau. 2013, January 18. "Drug Control Strategy and Policy." Retrieved June 27, 2013, from Narcotics Control Bureau, Government of India: http://narcoticsindia.nic.in/Drugcontrolstra.htm.

National Informatics Centre, Cooch Behar District Centre. 2002. Cooch Behar District Profile. Retrieved January 1, 2013, from *Geography*: http://coochbehar.nic.in/htmfiles/dist_summaryprofile.html#geography.

New Delhi Television Limited. 2011, February 9. "India to lose 10,000 acres in land swap deal with Bangladesh." Retrieved June 16, 2013, from NDTV: http://www.ndtv.com/article/india/india-to-lose-10-000-acres-in-land-swap-deal-with-bangladesh-84245.

New York Daily News. 2013, March 11. "Proposed enclave exchange with Bangladesh will be national loss: BJP." Retrieved July 4, 2013, from *New York Daily News*: http://india.nydailynews.com/newsarticle/80c7f6d4cefd5c2499c4797cccdfba00/proposed-enclave-exchange-with-bangladesh-will-be-national-loss-bjp.

News.az. 2012, March 7. "Azerbaijan, Iran, Turkey sign Nakhchivan declaration." Retrieved June 16, 2013, from News.az: http://news.az/articles/politics/56194.

Niyazova, M. 2013, May 29. "Barak enclave residents ask Kyrgyz officials to speed up problems' settlement." Retrieved June 29, 2013, from 24.kg: http://eng.24.kg/community/2013/05/29/27090.html.

Nuttall, C. 2013, January 22. "South Kyrgyzstan remains tense after Sokh violence." Retrieved June 30, 2013, from Business News Europe: http://www.bne.eu/story4436/South_Kyrgyzstan_remains_tense_after_Sokh_violence.

O'Ballance, E. 1957. "The Battle of Plassey, 1757." *Royal United Service Institution Journal*, 102, 363-71.

Padgett, R. B. 2013, July 3. Information Officer, Public Affairs Section, US Embassy in Tashkent, Uzbekistan. Personal email.

Pandey, A. 2011, September 12. "Hope for Indo-Bangladesh enclaves." Retrieved June 24, 2013, from New Delhi Television News: http://www.ndtv.com/article/india/hope-for-indo-bangladesh-enclaves-132956.

Panico, P. 2009. "San Marino: private foundations—a hidden secret?" Trusts and Trustees, 15:5, 403-5.

Passon, D. and A. Temirkulov. 2004, April. "Analysis of Peace and Conflict Potential in Batken Oblast, Kyrgyzstan." Retrieved June 24, 2013, from International Policy Fellowships: www.policy.hu/temirkulov/index.files/ARC_GTZ-Report-Kyrgyzstan.pdf.

Polat, A. and N. Butkevich. 2000. "Unravelling the mystery of the Tashkent bombings: Theories and implications." Demokratizatsiya, 8:4, 541-53.

Polgreen, L. 2011, October 9. "At India-Bangladesh Border, Living in Both, and Neither." Retrieved January 2, 2013, from *The New York Times*: http://www.nytimes.com/2011/10/10/world/asia/at-india-bangladesh-border-living-in-both-and-neither.html?pagewanted=all.

Poplin, C. 2013. "India and Bangladesh: A Review of Bilateral Opportunities and Constraints." Retrieved June 6, 2013, from Centre for Policy Research, Indian Development Cooperation Research (IDCR): http://idcr.cprindia.org/p/blog-page_6630.html.

Public Health and Engineering Department. 2012, April. "Mission & Vision." Retrieved June 26, 2013, from Public Health and Engineering Department, Government of West Bengal: http://www.wbphed.gov.in/main/Static_pages/mission.php.

———. 2012, April. "Water Quality Standards." Retrieved June 26, 2013, from Public Health and Engineering Department, Government of West Bengal: http://www.wbphed.gov.in/main/Static_pages/water_quality_standards.php, 2012.

Pylenko, Z. 2005, February 11. "Batken's Border Problems." Retrieved June 15, 2013, from *The Central Asia-Caucasus Analyst*: http://cacianalyst.org/publications/field-reports/item/10417-field-reports-caci-analyst-2005-11-2-art-10417.html.

Radio Free Europe/Radio Liberty. 2011, May 12. "Kyrgyz In Exclave In Uzbekistan Want To Relocate To Kyrgyzstan." Retrieved December 21, 2012, from Radio Free Europe/Radio Liberty: http://www.rferl.org/content/kyrgyz_in_exclave_want_to_relocate_to_kyrgyzstan/24099108.html.

Radio Free Europe/Radio Liberty. 2011, August 4. "Kyrgyzstan Allocates Land For Kyrgyz From Exclave In Uzbekistan." Retrieved December 21, 2012, from Radio Free Europe/Radio Liberty: http://www.rferl.org/content/kyrgyzstan_sets_aside_land_for_kyrgyz_from_uzbek_exclave/24286695.html.

Radio Free Europe/Radio Liberty. 2003, February 22. "Prime Minister Tanayev Meets with Residents of Barak Village." Retrieved July 6, 2013, from Kyrgyzstan Development Gateway: http://eng.gateway.kg/news/kyrgyzstan/society/1968.

Radio Free Europe/Radio Liberty. 2013, January 18. "Tajikistan Requests Documents

On Borders From Russia." Retrieved June 22, 2013, from Radio Free Europe/Radio Liberty: http://www.rferl.org/content/tajikistan-requests-documents-borders-russia/24877111.html.

Rahimov, M. and G. Urezaeva. 2005, March. "Central Asian Nations & Border Issues." Retrieved June 14, 2013, from Conflict Studies Research Centre: mercury.ethz.ch/serviceengine/Files/ISN/92527/.../en/05_Apr.pdf.

Rahman, M. A., M. Murshed and N. Sultana. 2013. "Lives outside the map: the case of Angarpota-Dahagram Enclave, Bangladesh." *IOSR Journal of Humanities and Social Science*, 9:1, 71-76.

Rashid, H. U. 2011, May 17. "Mamata Banerjee's victory in West Bengal and its impact on Bangladesh." Retrieved June 24, 2013, from http://www.priyoaustralia.com.au/articles/96271-mamata-banerjee%E2%80%99s-victory-in-west-bengal-and-its-impact-on-bangladesh.html.

Reina, P. 1993. "Huge project is launched in a tiny mountain kingdom." *Engineering News-Record*, 230:4, 26.

Republic of Azerbaijan Ministry of Foreign Affairs. (n.d.). "Economy, Nakhchivan Autonomous Republic." Retrieved June 16, 2013, from Republic of Azerbaijan, Ministry of Foreign Affairs, Nakhchivan Autonomous Republic: http://dmfa.nakhchivan.az/page.php?lang=eng&page=000108.

———. (n.d.). "Tourism, Nakhchivan Autonomous Republic." Retrieved June 16, 2013, from Republic of Azerbaijan, Ministry of Foreign Affairs, Nakhchiban Autonomous Republic: http://dmfa.nakhchivan.az/page.php?lang=eng&page=000109.

Sahlins, P. 1998. "State formation and national identity in the Catalan borderlands during the eighteenth and nineteenth centuries." In T. M. Wilson and H. Donnan, *Border Identities: Nation and State at International Frontiers*. Cambridge: Cambridge University Press, 31-61.

Samanta, P. D. 2012, June 3. "First Teesta, now Mamata objects to enclaves pact: Fear Bangla influx." Retrieved January 2, 2013, from *The Indian Express*: http://www.indianexpress.com/news/first-teesta-now-mamata-objects-to-enclaves-pact-fear-bangla-influx/957253.

Sarkar, D. 2012. "Economic Status of Enclave Dwellers: A Case Study of Poaturkuthi, Cooch Behar, India." *Indian Streams Research Journal*, 2:1, 1-4.

———. 2013, April 22. "Resolve Indo-Bangladesh bilateral issues using Enclave exchange accord: BJP to Government." Retrieved June 16, 2013, from *The Economic Times*: http://articles.economictimes.indiatimes.com/2013-04-22/news/38736119_1_teesta-indo-bangla-india-and-bangladesh.

Sattar, M. 2012, March 29. "Bangladesh-India: hunger strike you haven't heard of." Retrieved June 24, 2013, from *Global Post*: http://www.globalpost.com/dispatch/news/regions/asia-pacific/india/120328/bangladesh-border-dispute-enclaves-hunger-strike.

———. 2012, January 18. "Inside India's 'Stateless' Headache." Retrieved June 20, 2013, from *The Diplomat*: http://thediplomat.com/2012/01/18/inside-india%E2%80%99s-%E2%80%9Cstateless%E2%80%9D-headache/.

Sengupta, D. 2013, May 29 & 30. "Origins, Conditions, and Politics of the India-Bangladesh Enclaves." (G. R. Hamburg, Interviewer.)

Sirohi, S. 2013, March 12. "The BJP's Bangladesh problem." Retrieved July 4, 2013, from *South Asia Monitor*: http://southasiamonitor.org/detail.php?type=n&nid=4804.

Sukhov, A. 2002, May 29. "Chinese ace in Uzbek sleeve." Retrieved June 6, 2013, from Kyrgyzstan Development Gateway: http://eng.gateway.kg/news/cacis/1189.

The Arunachal Pioneer. 2013, March 23. "Both India and Bangladesh need to fathom the long run impacts before swapping land." Retrieved June 22, 2013, from *The Arunachal Pioneer*: http://www.thearunachalpioneer.in/editorial-posts/2013/03/23/both-india-and-bangladesh-need-to-fathom-the-long-run-impacts-before-swapping-land/.

The Daily Star. 2012, June 11. "Indo-Bangla enclave people at Mamata's door." Retrieved June 24, 2013, from *The Daily Star*: http://archive.thedailystar.net/newDesign/news-details.php?nid=237795.

———. 2011, September 9. "Tin Bigha now open for 24 hrs." Retrieved June 27, 2013, from *The Daily Star*: http://archive.thedailystar.net/newDesign/news-details.php?nid=201721.

The Economist. 2002, February 23. "Gibraltar in reverse? Spain's North African enclaves." *The Economist*, 362:8261, p. 72.

———. 2006, November 11. "Mountain rigger: Tajikistan's presidential election." *The Economist*, 381:8503, p. 76.

———. 2010, June 19. "Stalin's harvest; The latest outbreak of violence in the ethnic boiling-pot of Central Asia will take generations to heal." *The Economist*, 395:8687, pp. 26-28.

———. 2010, June 19. "Stalin's latest victims; The Kyrgyzstani government deserves help in dealing with history's dangerous legacy." *The Economist*, 395:8687, p. 15.

———. 2011, September 7. "The end of the enclaves." Retrieved June 16, 2012, from *The Economist*: http://www.economist.com/blogs/banyan/2011/09/border-agreements.

———. 2012, March 24. "Unfished journey; Indian politics." *The Economist*, 402:8777, pp. 27-30.

The Financial Express. 2011, September 7. "Dhaka wants explanation for postponing Teesta deal." *The Financial Express*.

The Globe and Mail. 1982, July 27. "San Marino rejects plan on citizenship." *The Globe and Mail*, p. 11.

The Hindu. 2013, March 3. "BJP won't support Bill to ratify India-Bangladesh border pact." Retrieved June 16, 2013, from *The Hindu*: http://www.thehindu.com/news/national/bjp-wont-support-bill-to-ratify-indiabangladesh-border-pact/article4469794.ece.

———. 2013, March 26. "Consensus emerging on statute change Bill." Retrieved June 16, 2013, from *The Hindu*: http://www.thehindu.com/news/national/consensus-emerging-on-statute-change-bill/article4551808.ece.

———. 2013, May 7. "Scuffle in Rajya Sabha over Bill to swap land with Bangladesh." Retrieved June 16, 2013, from *The Hindu*: http://www.thehindu.com/news/national/scuffle-in-rajya-sabha-over-bill-to-swap-land-with-bangladesh/article4692166.ece.

The Indian Express. 2013, February 6. "Budget Session of Parliament from February 21."

Retrieved June 16, 2013, from *The Indian Express*: http://www.indianexpress.com/news/budget-session-of-parliament-from-february-21/1070323/.

The Lithuanian Tribune. 2012, October 19. "Lithuanian-Belarusian border: Divided villages, divided lives." Retrieved July 10, 2013, from *The Lithuanian Tribune*: http://www.lithuaniatribune.com/17622/lithuanian-belarusian-border-divided-villages-divided-lives-201217622/.

The New York Times. 1959, June 14. "San Marino Asks No Aid: Official From Tiny Enclave in Italy Pays Visit to US." *The New York Times*, p. 38.

The Shillong Times. 2013, May 9. "AGP burns PM's effigy over land swap pact with B'desh." Retrieved June 16, 2013, from *The Shillong Times*: http://www.theshillongtimes.com/2013/05/09/agp-burns-pms-effigy-over-land-swap-pact-with-bdesh/.

The Telegraph. 2013, May 8. "Bangla bill seized from Khurshid." Retrieved June 16, 2013, from *The Telegraph*: http://www.telegraphindia.com/1130508/jsp/nation/story_16872885.jsp.

The Times of Central Asia. 2013, May 30. "Eurasian specialist warns that Central Asia's ethnic enclaves are 'heating up.'" Retrieved June 16, 2013, from Stratrisks: http://stratrisks.com/geostrat/12926?utm_source=feedburner&utm_medium=feed&utm_campaign=Feed%3A+StratRisks+%28StratRi sks%29.

The Times of India. 2013, April 23. "BJP must not stand in the way of Land Boundary Agreement between India and Bangladesh." Retrieved June 28, 2013, from *The Times of India*: http://articles.timesofindia.indiatimes.com/2013-04-23/edit-page/38762463_1_land-boundary-agreement-lba-constitution-amendment-bill.

———. 2013, June 29. "BJP to hoist national flag on proposed land for swap." Retrieved July 4, 2013, from *The Times of India*: http://articles.timesofindia.indiatimes.com/2013-06-29/guwahati/40271166_1_land-boundary-bangladesh-boroibari.

Trilling, D. 2013, January 21. "Kyrgyzstan & Uzbekistan: Border Crisis Enters Third Week." Retrieved June 24, 2013, from Eurasianet.org: http://www.eurasianet.org/node/66432.

Turgayev, S. 2013, February 12. "Tour to the ends of the earth." Retrieved June 29, 2013, from 24.kg: http://eng.24.kg/community/2013/02/12/25917.html.

UNDP in the Kyrgyz Republic. 2011. "Border Management in Central Asia." Retrieved June 16, 2013, from United Nations Development Programme in the Kyrgyz Republic: http://www.undp.kg/en/what-we-do/regional-cooperation/bomca.

———. 2011. "Peace and Development Programme," Project ID: 00046724, 00046724, 00056155. Retrieved June 16, 2013, from United Nations Development Programme in the Kyrgyz Republic: http://www.undp.kg/en/resources/project-database/article/1-projects/871-peace-and-development-programme.

United Nations. 2013. "Millennium Goals." Retrieved June 28, 2013, from United Nations: http://www.un.org/millenniumgoals/.

Upadhyay, V. 2011. "Water Rights and the 'New' Water Laws in India: Emerging Issues and Concerns in a Rights Based Perspective." India Infrastructure Report, 56-66.

Utyaganova, M. 2001, September 5. "Enclave Politics Between Bishkek and Tashkent Poison Relations." Retrieved June 16, 2013, from Central Asia-Caucasus Institute: http://old.cacianalyst.org/?q=node/472.

Van Schendel, W. 2002. "Stateless in South Asia: The Making of the India-Bangladesh Enclaves." *The Journal of Asian Studies*, vol. 61, no. 1, 115-47.

———. 2005. *The Bengal Borderland*. London: Wimbeldon Publishing Company.

Vinokurov, E. 2007. *A Theory of Enclaves*. Lanham: Lexington Books.

WaterAid. 2011, March. "Country Strategy Plan: 2011-2016, Bangladesh." Retrieved June 24, 2013, from WaterAid: www.wateraid.org/~/media/Publications/WaterAid-bangladesh-strategy.pdf.

West Bengal Police. (n.d.). "About Us." Retrieved June 27, 2013, from West Bengal Police, Government of West Bengal: http://policewb.gov.in/wbp/about-us.php.

Whyte, B. R. 2002. "Waiting for the Esquimo: An historical and documentary study of the Cooch Behar enclaves of India and Bangladesh." Doctoral Thesis Research Paper. Melbourne, Victoria, Australia: The School of Anthropology, Geography and Environmental Studies, The University of Melbourne.

Xinhua News Agency. 2010, September 27. "Azerbaijan says capable of exporting more natural gas to Iran." Xinhua News.

Zaman, R. U. 2012. "Bangladesh—Between Terrorism, Identity and Illiberal Democracy: The Unfolding of Tragic Saga." *Perceptions*, XVII:3, 151-177.

Zia, B. K. 2012. "Bangladesh-India Relations, Challenges and Prospects." *Strategic Analysis*, 36:5, 720-22.